In the Currents of Quiet

Sarah Carlson

Meanderings Publications
2020

Meanderings Publications
Farmington, Maine
meanderingspublications@gmail.com
https://meanderingsoftheheart.blogspot.com/

Cover & Interior Design: Höhne-Werner Design, www.heyneon.com

First Printing 2020

ISBN 978-0-578-64270-3

All photographs were taken by Sarah Carlson except the following, which are used with permission:

Emma Carlson
Water
Magical
Sea of Love
Soft Around the Edges
Light–Within and Without

Tom McAllister
Moments of Joy

Judith Aldrich
Artwork for Mother Love

Jake Risch
Sweet Safety Deepened
Lesson From a Southern Snake

Liz Koucky
Nothing to Do

Rami Haddad
Unique and Yet the Same

Katharina Burdet
Truth

Sheryl Farnum
To Be Sure

Terry Owens
Breathe Deep the Gathering Bloom

Katherine Carlson
Author Photo

The photo for *Oh How I Miss* was a wedding gift from Tade and Nancy Mahoney. One of them took the picture in the spring of 1979 when Barry and I stopped by to tell them we were getting married.

The following are family photos:

Marvel with Me—most likely taken by my father, George Terry, in 1958

Yesteryear and *Dear Me*—taken by a random skier who happened to be walking by the Sugarloaf trail map and was asked to take the picture by my parents. I believe that was in 1964.

In memory of Barry Francis Carlson

Dedicated to our children, Jence and Emma,
and their spouses, Katherine and Jake

Contents

Preface

As I shared my first book, *The Radiance of Change*, I was often asked how I began writing poetry. Though I have always enjoyed writing, often wrote poetry as a child, and had a literature minor as I pursued a teaching degree, I did not formally study the writing of poetry. My poetic voice emerged, and needed to be recognized, as part of my process of healing from the sudden death of my husband, Barry, in May of 2002.

Here's a piece of prose that I wrote as a way to describe how that voice came to the surface:

How It Began
May 25, 2002—the day before my 45th birthday and 2 days after his 60th. Moon Phase—full. Weather—clear and warm.
We walked along the well-worn path through the woods behind our house with our son. His younger sister was peacefully sleeping on the couch after winning the shot put in a track meet earlier in the day. We sat at our special spot by the river, moonlight shimmering from one bank to the other. Two Canada geese landed in the reflected light as we watched in awe. We later talked about those moments, recognizing what a truly spiritual experience it had been, how we believed that nature was our temple.
Four days later, he died while playing tennis with good friends. For a few years I kept forging ahead, busy with children transitioning from high school to college and teaching second graders. I walked and processed, feeling the most comfortable in the natural world. Over time, however, I had a growing understanding that I needed to begin healing more intentionally. More and more I noticed gentle metaphoric moments while watching clouds, spotting birds, examining the play of light on water, finding heart rocks at the most opportune times. I often took pictures of those serendipitous scenes.
As I turned inward and began exploring the multi-faceted layers of my inner world that clearly needed healing, words began to emerge in my own style of poetry. I soon realized that my writings and photographs were linked and so began pairing them together.
All along I felt as if the words came through me and for me, but that some day I would share at least some of them in the hopes they would aid others in healing. My first book, The Radiance of Change, *is a culmination of 12 years of poetry and photography with 175 pairings of the two. A culmination, though I am not finished, as the writing still comes just when I need it. I write the poetry, though in truth it is writing me.*

April 22, 2018

I continue to have the sense that the poetry is writing me. This is combined with a deep and lively recognition of how my years of teaching also come into play. I know the words that come have so much to teach. That's what drives the desire to share and paves the way for taking the huge step of again putting a book into the world.

This book, I believe, represents a shift from healing to embracing health. I've discovered that finding a sense of wellness is really about accessing and feeling comfort in what is true in the moments of one's life. Only we know what is real for us, what resonates within. Only we can decide what to do with the emotions that arise, sensations that occur, challenges that exist. Only we can make the choice to move into healing and explore what might help us be well. That's what health means to me—the capacity to be true to my own experience, explore my own feelings without judgment, say what I need to say while trusting my own wisdom, pause when necessary, forge ahead when the time is right.

In the preface of my first book I described the healing modalities that I have discovered work well for me. Those being osteopathy, spiritual direction, counseling, and massage. I realized after publication that I left out one other important aspect of my work—mindfulness.

I discovered mindfulness about four years ago as I was taking a yoga private with Jeri Wilson of School Street Yoga in Waterville, Maine. I had gone to her for help in designing a yoga sequence that I could use in the morning before heading to my work as a fourth grade teacher. The stress of the school day was wearing me down a bit more than in the past. I felt that being more specific in preparing for the day would help me be fully present for my students. During that private Jeri asked me if I had ever thought of using meditation as part of my morning routine. I chuckled as I responded, "Sure, I think of it often. But, I've never been one to sit still for very long." She smiled and encouraged me to try sitting in silence for a few minutes each morning. Her advice, combined with the sense of connection I felt between us in those moments, helped me know it was time to explore quiet. Since then mindfulness has become part of everyday life, weaving its way into my poetry and my teaching.

All of the above has led to that shift of being more and more in my health, experiencing my own vigor. That's not to say that I don't have aches and pains, challenges and unease. The difference is that I can simply be more at ease with life as it unfolds. I can notice, explore, ponder, pause, learn, and teach just as I am right here, right now. I know that following my heart is a reliable way to go, that meanders will provide the insights I need in the right way, at the right time. Things will unfurl as they will and I can trust my own responses along the way. From experiencing moments of radiance as I adapted to change to feeling aglow with the sparkling energy of health, I'm excited to share this new collection of poetry.

While word choice is important, especially to a poet, it's really the essence of our experiences that matters. I hope that the nature of the words within these pages resonates with you and helps you find moments of stillness, currents of quiet, where clarity crystallizes in whatever way you may need in your own times of exploration and growth.

After the publication of *The Radiance of Change*, I realized that I hadn't really included any mention of my brother's death. My only sibling, Geof, died in a bicycle accident in 1987 at the age of 33. As I pondered that, I realized that I had actually been processing that loss through my writing, too. This time around that came through more strongly and I have thought about my big brother often as I put this book together. He, who would now be a grandfather to two adorable little girls.

Another thing that came back around were some aspects about my father and his death. Ever my biggest fan, including encouraging me to publish over the years, he has been in my heart through the publishing process this time, too. So, here's to two other family members who are gone, but whose love remains—George F. Terry IV and George F. Terry III.

With continued gratitude to:
Daniel Gibbons, D.O. The Reverend Ann Kidder, M.Div., S.T.M.
Jonathan M. Borkum, Ph.D. Terry K. Owens, B.S., L.M.T.

Along with thanks to the readers of and listeners to *The Radiance of Change*, my family, my friends, and all the amazing children I have shared time with over the years.

I'd like to close by expressing my thanks to Angela Werner of Höhne-Werner Design, my book designer and editor. Her gentle guidance has been a welcome part of the process, both with this book and with my first. She let me take the lead, but knew when to offer suggestions along the way. This book is my creative endeavor, a crucial part of my healing and wellness, and she let it be so with both professionalism and kindness.

—Sarah Carlson

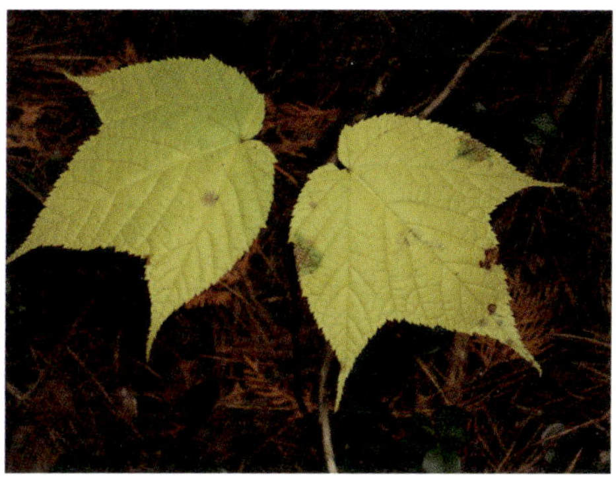

The Boots

There, amidst the unused clothes,
beckoned the boots.
Constant reminder of the physical loss.
Embodiment of who he was—
lover, rebel, father, cowboy, soulmate.
They called out—what about me?
What are you going to do with me, without me?
There they lay—unfilled, moldy, sorrowful.
Yet, were they him?
Or were they just something he cherished?
Some THING that had value to him, but were no longer needed.
No longer needed because he is in us—in every life he touched.
Clearly in me—his loving wife.
Clearly in the children he so cherished and who inspired awe in him.
His footprints are indelibly etched in our hearts,
in our souls, in who we are.
No longer are the boots needed.
We are going on to make our own footprints,
walking our own paths,
but carrying him with us, each in our own way.
Moving to the rhythms of our memories, his laughter, his love.
The boots are gone, but he is not.

August 2006

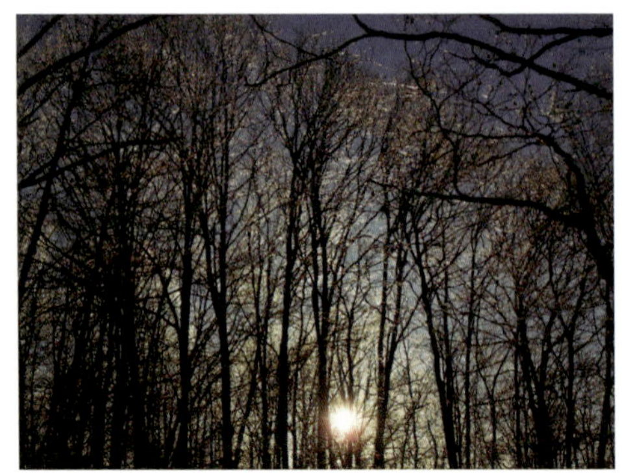

Remember the Love

A quiet house
once full of laughter and love.
Echoes of what was filling my mind.
Their excitement and joy,
his calm reassurance.
Where have they gone,
my family, my core?
This place, this home,
once so happy and full.
So very different now,
and yet the same.
Is the love still there—
in my heart, in my soul?
Silence becomes sadness
in my disjointed brain.
The quiet stirs doubt,
the doubt begets fear.
How can I bear it,
this new way to be?
Just me on my own
for the very first time.
I must remember the love—
in my heart, in my soul.
For it does help define me,
what I've lived, who I've been.
And it can sustain me
in what will come now.
If I can remember the love—
in my heart, in my soul.

September 2006

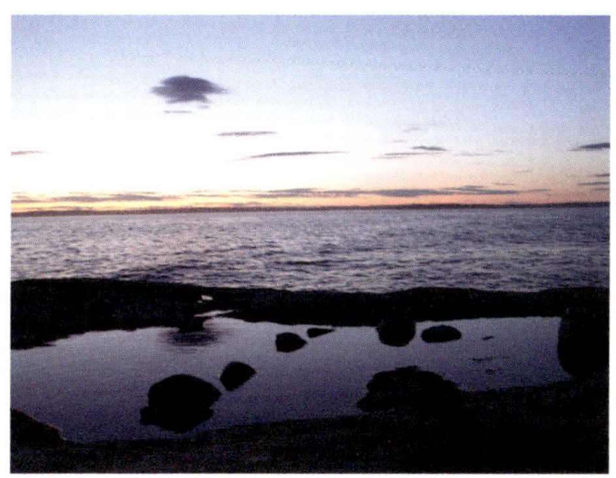

Water

Ocean waves rolled onto beaches
as we walked hand in hand,
watching the sun seem to slip into the deep.
Whitecaps crashed, yet beckoned us
onto the lake to try the wind
in our sweet little Sunfish.
Fog rose from the still surface
as we sat in the motor boat
that cradled us as you tempted the fish.
River in motion, flowing past our home.
How many times, how many ways,
did we make the trip from bridge to bridge?
Lakeside campsite on our island paradise.
Sunrises, sunsets, moonbeams reflected
as we marveled at the beauty of it all.
And that very last time at our spot by the river,
babbling brook providing a musical background,
our friends the geese sharing the moment.
We met by the lake nestled
at the foot of our mountain.
Adventures galore as we formed our bond.
Family outings in canoes, kayaks,
at every stage of our children's lives.
Oceans, lakes, rivers, streams.
Water always a part of
who we were, what we had.
Perhaps that's why when the river speaks
I know to listen.

December 28, 2006

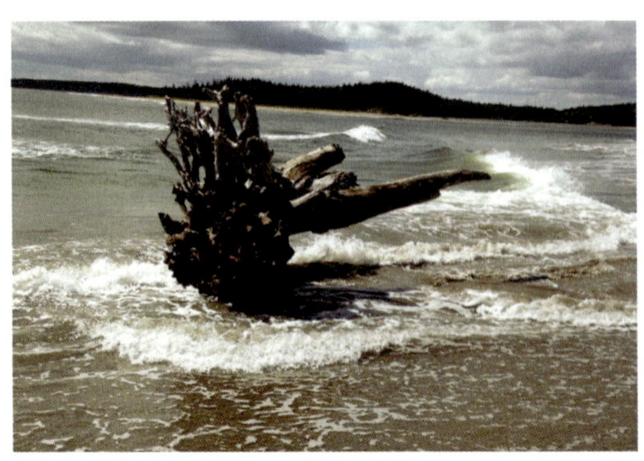

The Grip

A gnarled hand had a firm grip on me
that represented childhood fears
anchored in the perceptions
of a wonderful little girl.
I didn't know I was afraid,
I just thought I was wrong,
inherently wrong.
As I turn and face
the losses and sorrows
of my life,
I peel back the fingers of
that gnarled hand
one by one.
Each one grounded in what was
my reality.
This grip produced a fear that has
at times been electric,
at times liquid,
coursing through my body,
taking negative, deceptive control.
I understand now that
before I can fully embrace
the inherent goodness
that has long been within,
I must respect the grip
that the gnarled hand had,
recognize it was
there for reasons I could
not have understood in the past.

As I do it will be
time for it to let go,
for me to fully break free,
hold my truth
gently, tenderly,
as I learn to take
positive, productive control.

December 30, 2006

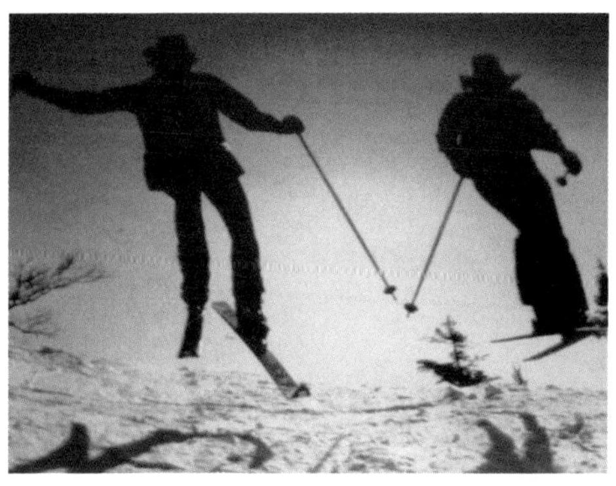

Moments of Joy

Walking in the rain on a foggy night,
dancing chamois shirt to chamois shirt,
hiking mountains simply for the view,
horseback-riding on a country road,
snuggling by a campfire
with no idea of the time.
Flying down a ski trail with
winter wind nipping our cheeks,
reaching the bottom
only to head back up for more.
Pounding tennis balls
back and forth for hours,
discussing technique, strategy,
but hardly ever the score.
Our garden wedding
on a beautiful June day,
eyes locked, hands held,
smiles and tears.
Holding our babies,

one son, one daughter,
marveling at every
stage of their growth.
Their walking, their talking,
their personalities unfolding.
So many family moments
to treasure and be retold.
And yes, that last special night by our river,
hanging out with our friends the geese
under the light of the full moon,
being together and feeling so very right.
These are the moments
that in my sadness, in my grief,
I forgot to remember
as moments of joy.

January 7, 2007

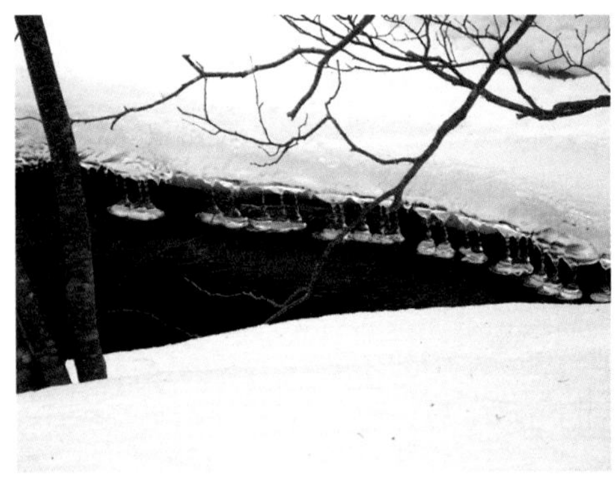

Lesson From a Wintry Brook

Purposeful brook making its way
through woods and fields,
around rocks and fallen trees,
to the river.
The brook had something to say today
as I walked along its banks.
I watched its course as it met the river.
Edges caked with slushy ice,
only the stronger current made it through.
As it merged with the water from the river
it curled back, swirling in indecision.

After some time it made its way,
went with the flow.
The merged waters harbored chunks of ice
that moved easily with the current,
just there to be carried until they melted
or were set down.
Purposeful little girl making her way
through happy times and desperate days
to adulthood.
Her edges frozen,
the strong currents of her courage
and her will have made it through.
She remains unsure at times,
but the goodness of who she was
is awakening in me
in a way that I can acknowledge.
We, together,
are understanding the pieces
of the load
we have been carrying.
Some we have melted,
others we have set down.
Purposeful little brook, purposeful little girl,
making their way,
moving on,
flowing into the unknown.

January 11, 2007

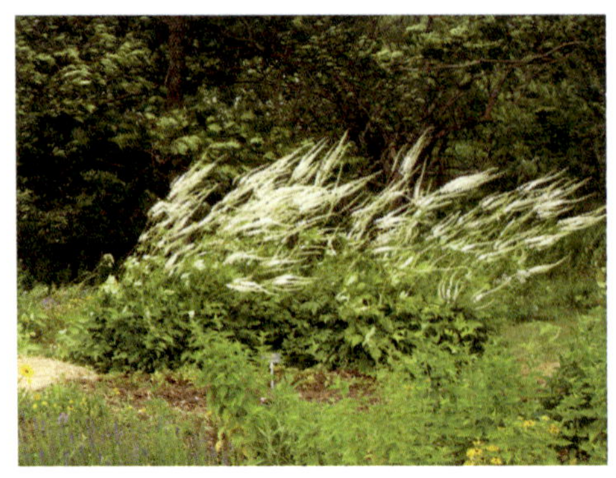

Winds of Change

Wind—movement, power, change.
Gentle breezes
tickle placid waters,
produce playful ripples
that interrupt the stillness,
stir grasses and leaves
into a lively dance,
lift newly-fallen snow into
swirls that frolic and settle
in new places
with fresh perspective.
Strong winds
toss majestic whitecaps,
can be harnessed by sail
and the knowledge
of how to steer a vessel,
bend and shake trees,
spread seeds for new life,
snap weaker limbs
that fall and become
fuel for new growth,
make waves of crystal flakes
leaving drifts and imprints
of the paths of change.
Updrafts, downdrafts, thermals,
air currents that ebb and flow
like my beloved river.
Dynamic—
at times peaceful,
other times powerful.

The winds of change are moving
around and through me,
taking away
discontent and despair,
helping to provide the understanding
of inner power,
the impetus for
change.

March 7, 2007

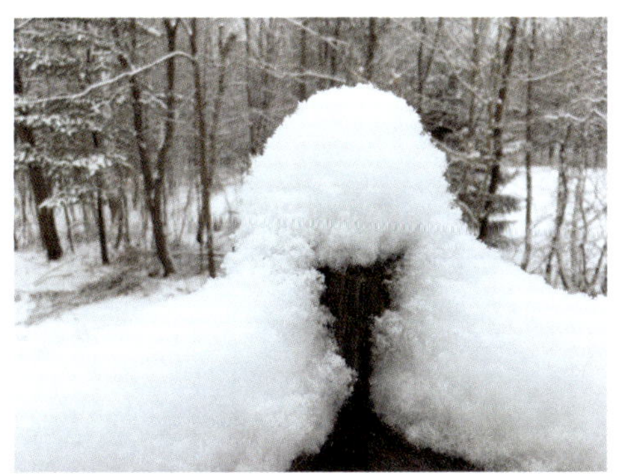

I'll Hold You

You don't want words,
not yet anyway.
I understand that.
Words represent
the possibility of emptiness
to you right now.
There were too many words
you didn't understand, were not true.
Words that were spoken in anger,
were not what
you deserved to hear.
You want to be held,
to reach out and
know that someone is there.
You want to feel it,
not hear it.
So, little one,
my hands are here.

Gentle hands of kindness,
hands of love.
My arms are here.
Caring arms of compassion,
arms of love.
I'll hold your little being
as you learn to relax and trust.
I'm here.
I'll hold you
so you can feel the love
and know it's real.
You are safe here with me.
I'll hold you.

March 26, 2007

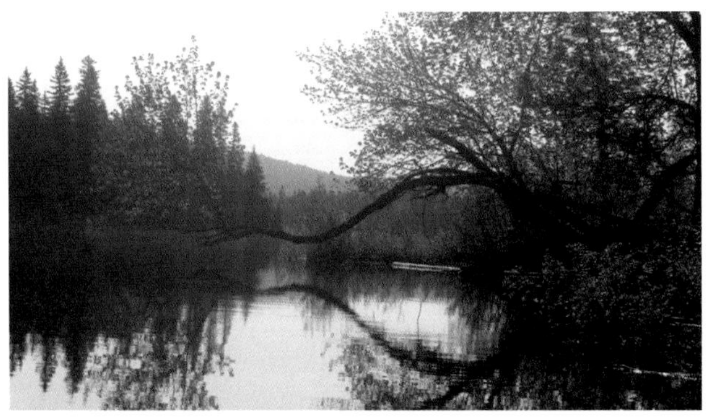

Magical

There once was a magical teacher.
Children she worked with
recognized her magic,
knew she understood them.
The magic was gentle and simple.
She valued them for who they were,
tapped into their inherent goodness,
often knew just the right
words to say,
helped them know it was
okay to let themselves flow.
It wasn't about facts and figures,
it was about the little moments

all through the day,
moments that showed her students
she saw the light within them all.
There once was a magical child
who was filled with goodness
and kindness and wisdom.
She was quick to help others,
but inwardly unsure about
her own true worth.
She walked through life
instinctively reaching out,
finding the positive in all
who shared her life.
Yet she didn't see the positives
within her own being,
was afraid to let herself flow.
One day the magical child met
the magical teacher
and began to understand
a simple lesson that only
the magical teacher could
help her learn.
She must look within
and give to herself that
which she so freely gave to others.
It was all there,
everything she needed.
She just needed to trust it
to find inner peace and joy.
Magical teacher, magical child—
Strong currents within me.
As they merge,
I begin to freely flow.

June 26, 2007

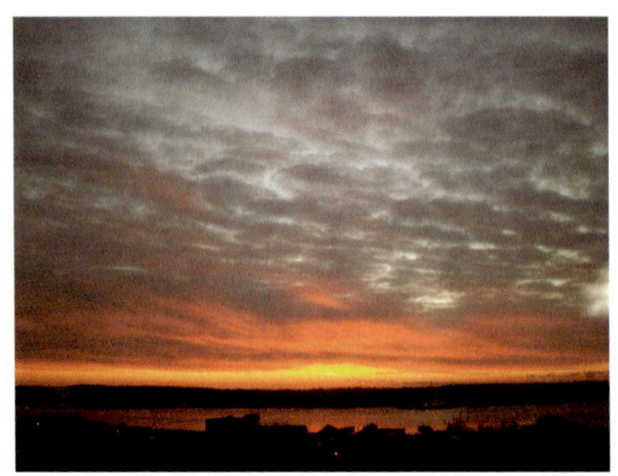

A New Day Dawns

Early morning grayness,
left over rainbursts
come and go.
Winds of change
work the higher clouds
as they twist and turn,
travel to new places.
Bits of blue peek
through the swirling masses
of dissipating vapor.
A new day dawns
as sunlight bathes
the treetops.
Dancing leaves
glow in the soothing newness,
spreading hope and the
promise of the light
working its way through
the darker layers
to the ground.

September 13, 2007

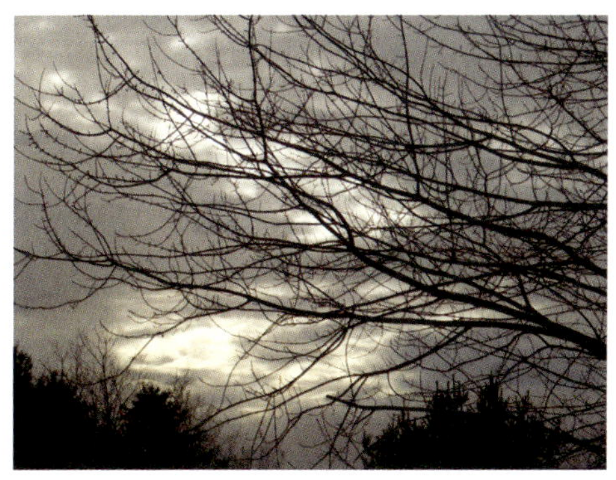

The Satchel

Old and worn,
leather thin and faded,
frayed strap stretched
with the weight of it all.
Every available space within
packed with old baggage
that is not yours to carry,
never should have been.
I can see it pulling on your right shoulder.
Your muscles strain with effort
as you steadfastly put
one foot in front of the other.
Your sweet face turns my way
and you look shyly into my eyes.
Questioning, wondering,
wanting to trust.
You listen as I lovingly tell you
that it's time to set it down,
release your grip and walk away.
You know I know how hard it has been
to take it all on,
how carefully and gallantly
you've borne the load.
Your little hands raise it from your shoulder.
You're weary and you let me help.
As we set it down at the side of our path
your fingers linger on the strap of
that old familiar satchel.
But I reach out my hand and you take it.
Then, it happens ...

You let me lift you up,
wrap your arms around my neck,
lean your head on my shoulder,
begin to relax.
I walk away with you in my arms.
Your little body quivers with emotion and energy
as we leave the satchel behind
and go forward with hope
in our heart.

November 16, 2007

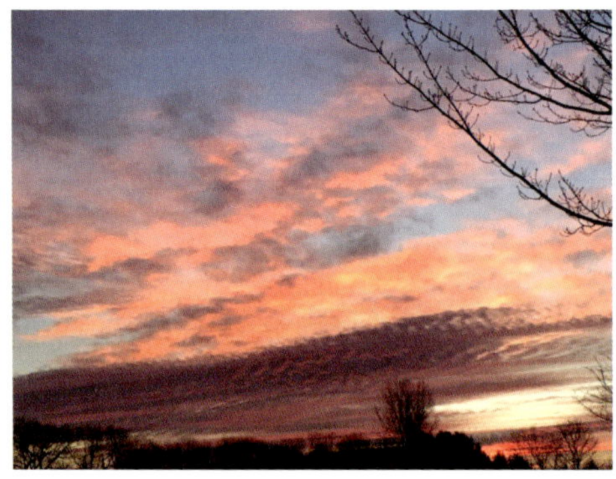

The Satchel Revisited

You're right little one.
We need to revisit the satchel.
I understand your need to
examine the contents—
hold them in your hands,
contemplate them in your mind,
honor them in your heart.
I never should have expected you
to just walk away
from something that you
carried for such a long time,
that represents so much
that was dark,
but that also contains
pieces of your light.
Your were not wrong to carry it.
In fact you are so noble

to have done so.
Your strength,
courage, purposefulness
are amazing.
But it's time for me to
be the one you turn to.
For you know, truly know,
that you are safe, respected,
and loved right here.
Are you ready?
Let's open up your
precious satchel
and decide together
what we need in order
to move ahead.

December 6, 2007

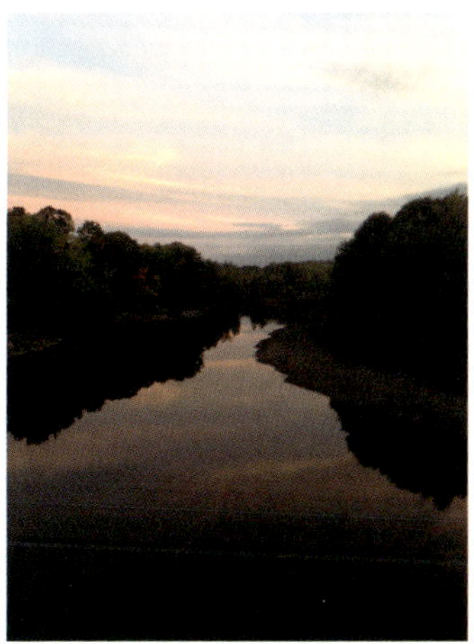

Little Girl Unfurled

Okay, little one, take my hand.
We're going to jump in together.
Trust me, it's really okay.
I will protect you—always.
It's your choice, but I think
we are ready.
So, if you want to, really want to,
grab on, take a deep breath,

and let's go.
There, I can feel you relaxing,
my little girl unfurled.
Ready?
1-2-3,
Yee-hah!!
Feel it?
We're flowing together—
safe, joyous, fearless.
The current, our current,
will take us
around meanders
to beautiful new vistas,
along restful stretches
where we can take time to
feel peace,
and into whitewater
where we can ride the waves
and feel the energy—together.

January 31, 2008

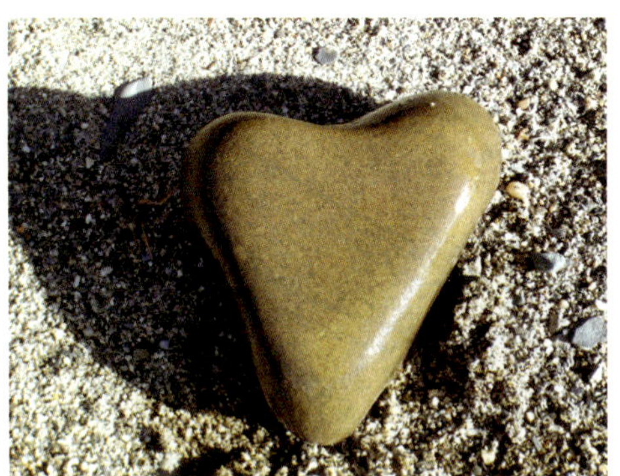

I Saw You

I saw you
in my new space.
I was afraid
you would think I
had erased you
as I took things apart
and sorted through me.

My love, our love,
is still strong,
but it's different now.
I can't touch you,
hold you, process things
with you.
But I had to make
this place mine.
And then there you were,
sitting back, relaxing
and smiling your wonderful smile.
Reassuring, approving,
supporting.
Just there in the space
as I need you to be.

February 22, 2008

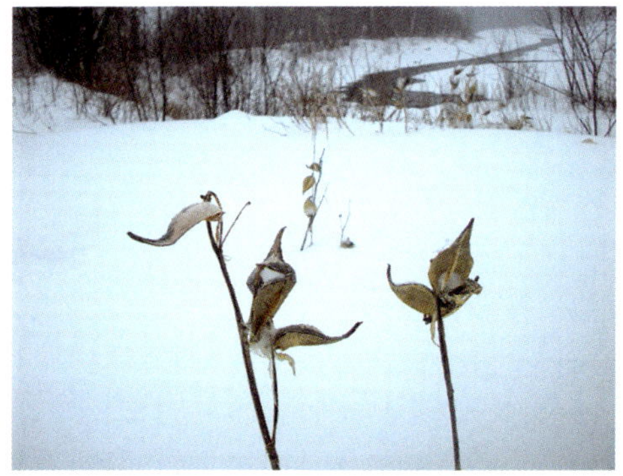

Good Sorrow

I never thought that sorrow
could be a good thing.
But, truthfully,
when it is felt for the purpose of release,
honored and not judged,
it is a very good thing.
Experiencing sorrow means
that you care about what was,
and, as importantly,
about what is.
It provides an outlet

for true grief to happen
as it should.
In going into the goodness
of sorrow,
one can find meaning
and solace
and love.
So I wish good sorrow
to all who have lost something
or someone.
Let it come,
let it go,
let it heal,
let it flow.
Good sorrow.

June 24, 2008

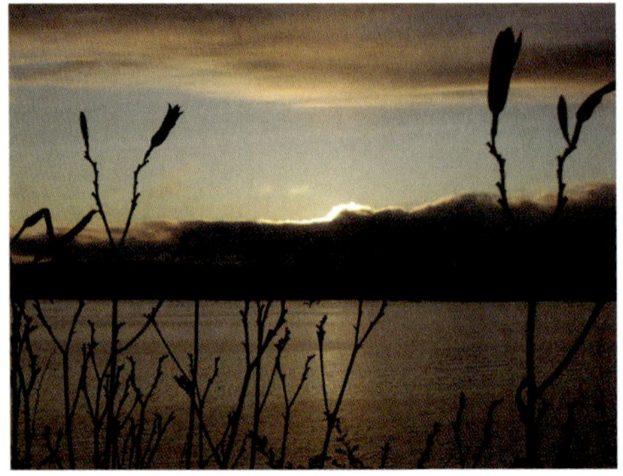

Unfurling

The layers unravel and reveal
innate beauty, her core.
Stretching, testing,
the rapture of her truth
buoys her and ...
suddenly she feels exposed,
vulnerable, unsafe.
Curling back upon herself
she thinks she is wrong, again.
The lure of her truth,
newly freed,

pulls at her, and she
relaxes and unfurls once more.
Ahhh there it is,
ecstasy, energy and love—
the ability to trust,
to be just as she is.
She feels it, thinks she is there,
and once again the old patterns
cause her to wither and curl.
But this time as she does,
she recognizes that something
is leaving, vaporizing into
the Universe, and she
understands her process
as a slow, gentle
unfurling as she learns to
simply be herself
in the moments of
her life.

July 11, 2008

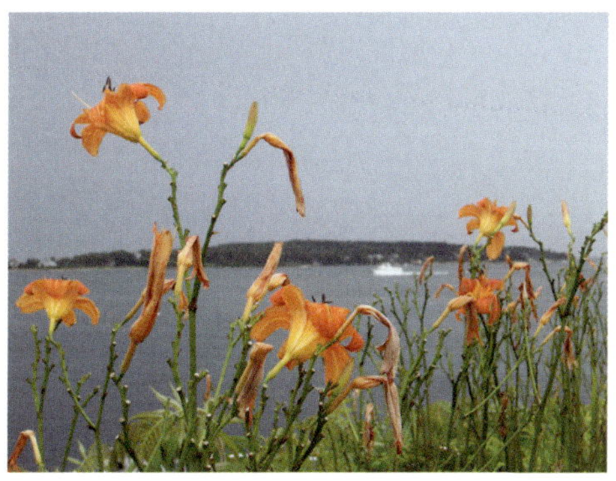

Enfolding

Like a rose she opens
to her world
anew.
Like a day lily
she curls in
at night.
Opening and closing she

tests, tries, tarries a while
when it feels
right.
Her eyes see things she
didn't recognize
before.
Her mind functions
more in tandem with
her heart.
She wraps her arms
around all that is
hers—
beautiful body,
open heart,
active mind,
loving soul.
Embracing all that is
within and without,
she knows that her gifts
are hers
to honor and share.
Enfolding—going in
to all that is good,
instead of going
away.

July 20, 2008

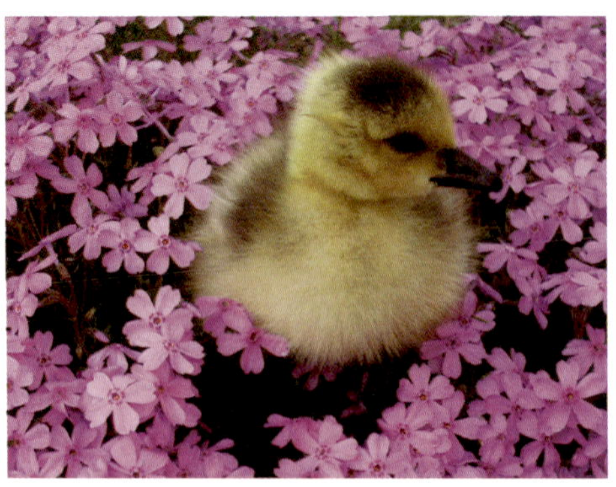

Perseverance

Baby bird, abandoned,
rides the flow of the brook.

Peeping his fear and
loneliness,
he sees a chance for help.
Making his way to shore,
he is challenged and threatened
by a creature larger than
himself.
He eludes the danger and
makes his way to the other side
to hide.
Knowing he cannot make it alone he
takes a chance and crosses the shallows—
drawn to the being he
somehow knows understands his needs.
He follows her,
tripping over rocks and roots,
instinctively trusting her worth.
She finds a way to help, and
in time,
he gains strength,
finds his voice,
fills out his body,
stretches his wings,
and is released to enjoy
the wild and
wonderful world.

August 24, 2008
inspired by Persy, a Canada gosling who followed
me home from Barker Brook on May 28, 2008

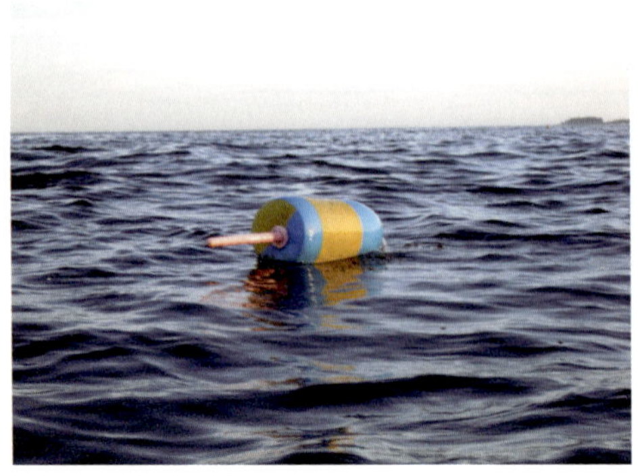

Sea of Love

Sweet being finds
her way in
to her inner core
of goodness.
Just a visit, perhaps,
but enough to validate
the purity of
who she really is.
A deep and full understanding
that it was never her fault
there was always something wrong,
leads to a sense that it truly is okay to
fill her own skin and simply feel right.
Pain and sorrow linger
as she bravely
continues her quiet and
caring battle to
reclaim her self.
This gentle warrior moves more
calmly and surely
into her future as
she learns that what she
taps within
and experiences without
are connected,
and that when she settles
and lets it all flow
she feels suspended in a

sea of love
and knows she belongs.

October 9, 2008

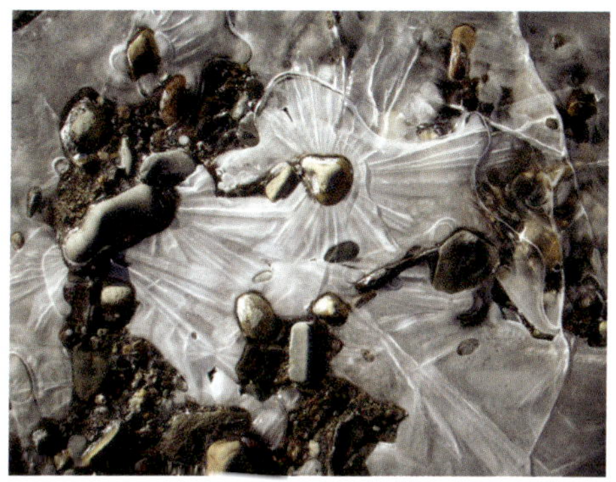

Slow Dance

Careful circles above the fray
provide perspective and distance,
room for reflection,
a bird's eye view with time
to twist the lens
for further acuity.
Each turn of this slow dance
makes way for more to unwind,
leading to relief and new insights.
Round and round—
circles cross and connect to
become interwoven,
creating a sweet, soft tapestry
that envelops a being
so that it is finally safe to let go
of all that no longer serves.
Settling into a new way to be,
freeing a true self,
feeling worthy of fully experiencing
the wonders of the universe.
Deep realization that
by trusting the connectedness,
feeling the love,
believing in the light,

it is safe and right
to spread strong, steady wings,
join the winds of change,
and soar.

January 15, 2009

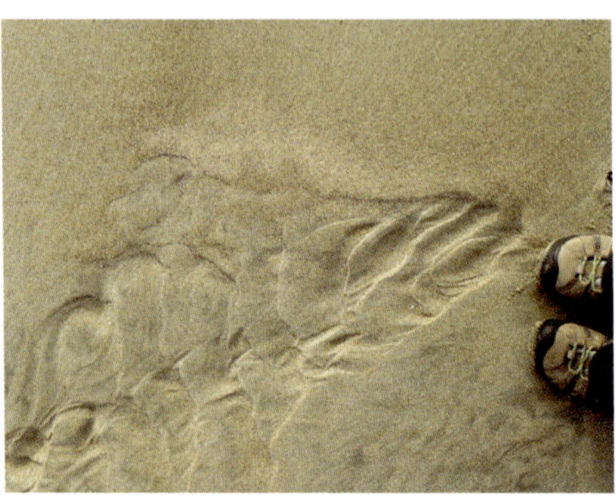

Where Does it Go?

Sometimes I feel remnants of fear,
but I'm not afraid.
When it happens I feel small,
but I am expansive.
In those moments I feel breathless,
but I can breathe.
The feeling washes through,
fills me for a time,
then lessens and fades away.
It makes me wonder,
where does it go?
If I release it,
can it hurt anyone else?
It comes like a wave
building to a crest,
then curling over and
gently spreading upon
a sandy beach that
absorbs and disperses its power.
So that must be where it goes.
It slips through the grains of sand,
bubbling and oozing to places

that can take it on.
Where does it go?
To places beyond my knowing,
where it no longer has the
power to make me hurt.
It's not mine anymore.
It may take some more time,
but I think I understand
that it is safe to let it go.
Where does it go?
It doesn't matter.
It just goes.

January 28, 2009

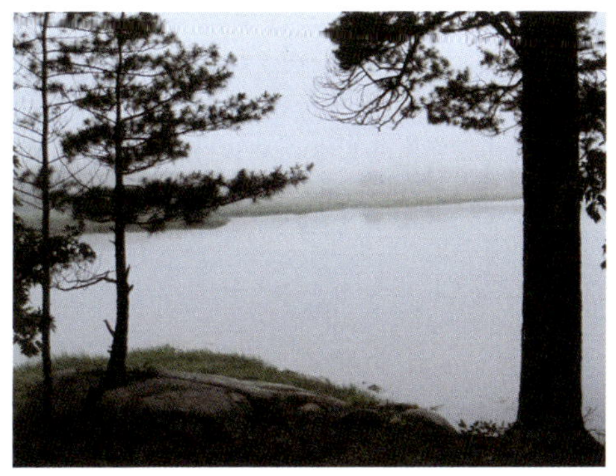

Soft Around the Edges

In letting go, breaking away,
I'm feeling hazy.
Not lost in the fog—
just nebulous, murky, vague.
Like the mist that
sometimes hovers over my
beloved river,
waiting for early morning light
to gently warm the vapors
left behind by the coolness
of the night.
Soft around the edges,
muffled and serene,
it lets go in wisps

that curl away,
seeming to disappear,
yet part of an ongoing cycle.
Water attracted to water,
a haze layered over the flow.
Not threatening or even definable,
simply there for a time.
But, as always, the river
knows where to go.
It doesn't question.
It just takes whatever comes
and continues along its way.
Another lesson to be learned.
I don't always need to know,
only to allow my self to flow.

July 21, 2009

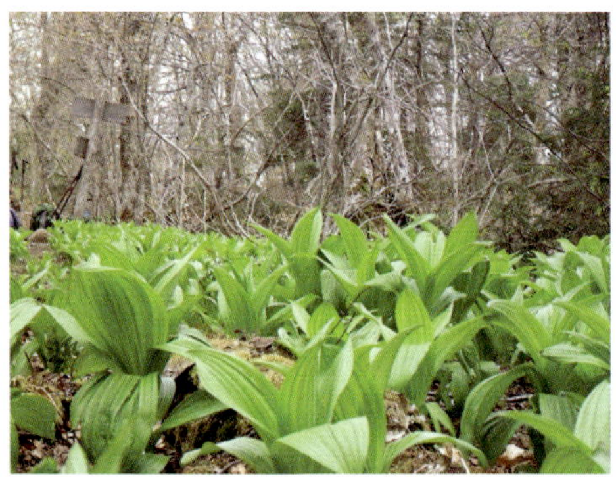

Joyful Birth

The child awaits,
suspended in a comfortable
liquid womb,
heart beating in unison
with mother's.
Energy shifts and the time comes
to leave the watery realm and
move into newness.
Mother's muscles pulsate with the
power of her core,
a rhythm like no other.

Driven by a knowing that comes
from both within and without,
mother and child work in tandem
to dance a dance
as old as time.
The baby's soft, pliable body
surges forth as the mother
harvests her labor and
releases a fresh life
into the world.
Together and separate,
a synthesis of beings,
mother and child stretch into
their bodies, reaching,
extending into an ecstasy of cells
unfolding, opening,
brimming with love.
A joyful birth that is right
and real and
richly deserved.

August 26, 2009

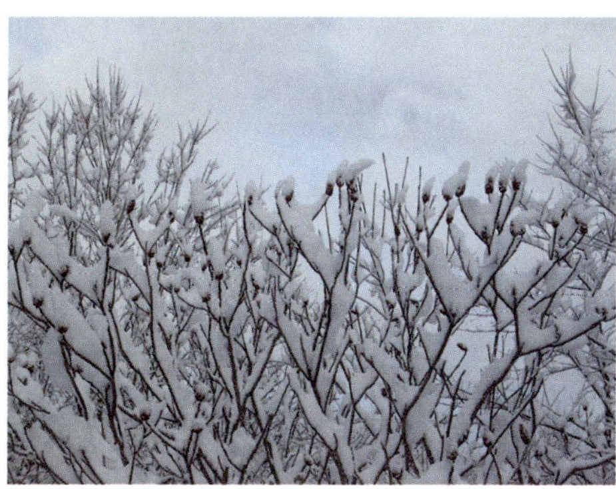

Solitary

Singular snowflakes waft down from above,
destined for a temporary perch on
bristly branches, silent structures,
weaving waterways, luscious landscapes,
furred or feathered friends.
Perfectly complete on their own as they descend,

the angles and edges of their forms
create an intricate, crystalline whole.
On their solitary journey there is
no need to struggle or resist.
They simply go where air currents take them,
trusting as they become
a part of another whole for a time,
then melt away
to eventually flow anew.

March 1, 2012

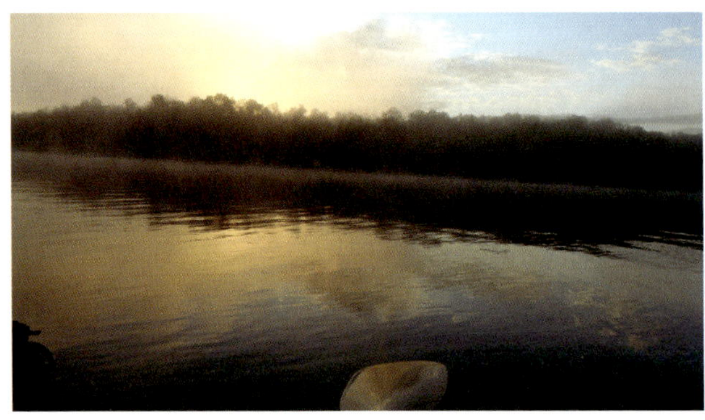

Light—Within and Without

Kayak slices through the waters
of a beloved river
as it meanders 'round rocks and trees
that dip from banks
eroded by the barrage.
Human skin soaks in the rays,
the being within smiles at the shift.
Inner radiance weaves its
way to the surface,
merges with
the beams from our nearest star—
reflecting,
refracting,
revealing,
releasing,
Light.

Warmth spreads about the misty morn
as water vapors reach for the sky.
New grasses sway in a gentle breeze,
shadows mimic the dance.
Whitewater ahead pulsates, gyrates,
beckons.
Kayak and human cavort as one,
follow the flow,
travel the torrent, then ...
bask in the warming glow—
reflecting,
refracting,
revealing,
releasing,
Light.

April 15, 2013

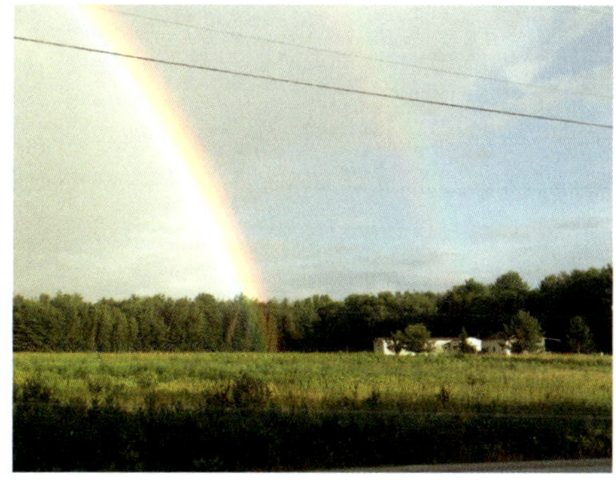

Have Faith

Through life's mountains, valleys,
and mill pond moments
I know now that I've had faith.
Sometimes as I slogged through the muck
I do admit that I wondered.
But there has always been a
protected, pristine place within
where belief in God lay in wait.
It emerged when I needed it,
but in ways that were not always
easy to recognize due to traumas

that warped my lens, skewed my perceptions,
and twisted my spirit.
Through carefully constructed defenses
I found love, and love found me.
Messages from the sky,
woods, and flowing waters
were delivered to me in times
of stress, despair, and loss.
I've battled stale learnings and vigilantly allowed
my self to set my defenses aside in order to heal.
As I tenderly look back I remember multiple times
when I stumbled, fell, or was cast aside,
but I cherish the benevolence with which
I forged ahead.
My strength, courage, and compassion
have long been in play.
I am learning to be more fully secure
in trusting my knowing.
And I know that,
both Within and Without,
I have faith.

July 5, 2015

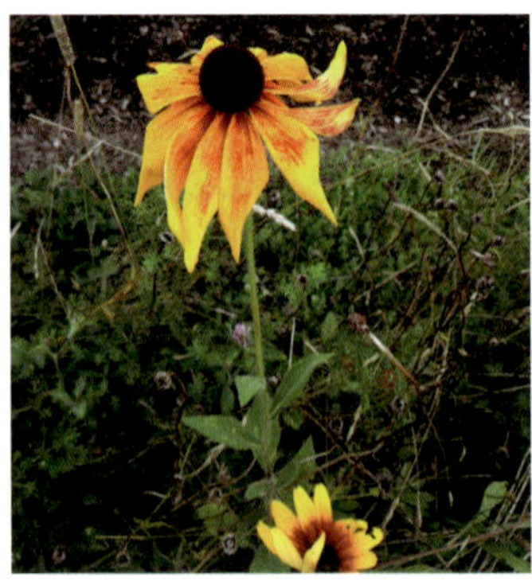

Tender Vulnerability

I feel her tender vulnerability as she searches
for answers in places tainted with hostility and pain.
Her innate determination shines as she puts one foot in front of the other
and warily explores the past.
Stagnant fear washes through her little body,

but she continues to walk around the old gray cabin by the lake.
Sunny kitchen, booze-filled pantry, breezy porch,
outdoor picnic area where kisses and hugs were bought and sold.
She walks down the stone stairs to the lakeshore,
pauses by the ancient, white canoe.
She looks at the keel of the overturned vessel,
remembering that her great-grandfather made it with his own hands,
sighing with the knowledge that there is so much she
doesn't know, doesn't understand about them.

I gently take her hand and we move to the edge of the water.
Again, I feel her tender vulnerability
as she takes a deep breath, holds on.
There's no one around and together we gaze upon the placid scene.
Her tenseness softens to a loose uneasiness and she looks into my eyes.
We're okay, little one, I say.
I've got you now. I love you.
She straightens up, expands, grows more full.
She spreads her arms out wide,
looks up into the soft clouds above.
I feel her relax, but know that she's still wary,
because I am, too.

It's true though, that the darkness is not really ours.
In time we will learn to trust
that it is all-the-way safe to be just as we are.
We didn't do anything wrong.
It was not our fault that so much was broken in those places.
We are here now together, growing and learning.
Soon we will walk stride for stride
as our tender vulnerability continues to mend.

July 22, 2015

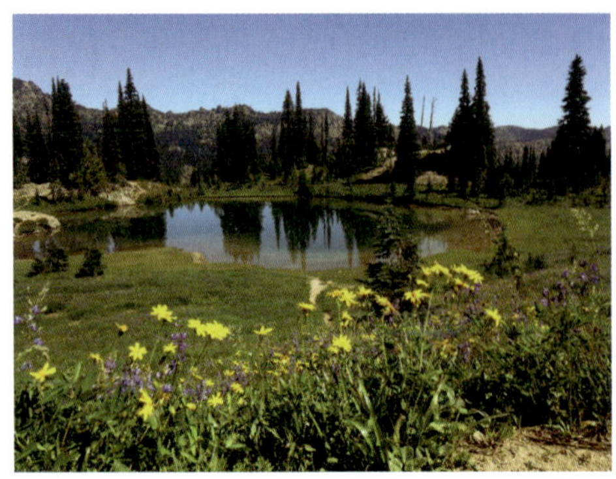

My Own Two Feet

Taking a full, deep breath I fill my lungs with
clean, crisp air.
My experienced, yet tender,
feet are firmly planted
on the sweet, solid earth below.
My wide-open eyes gaze upon glorious mountains
in the distance and reflective waters nearby.
Grasses sway in a gentle breeze as
wildflowers pulsate with color and happiness.
Mystical swirls of water vapor form
fair weather clouds in the radiant blue sky.
Tears begin to work their way to the surface,
representing hard work, deep exploration,
amazing shifts, residual confusion.
In this moment, though, I softly brush them aside.
This is a time to savor, celebrate,
and I can cry later.
I reach my arms out wide, wanting to embrace
all that is,
all that was,
all that will be.
There's more to do, more to know,
more to grow.
But I'm okay, we're okay.
We're becoming one
as we move into wholeness.
I'm standing on my own two feet,
right here,
right now,

grateful for my gifts, my life,
happy to be me.

August 5, 2015

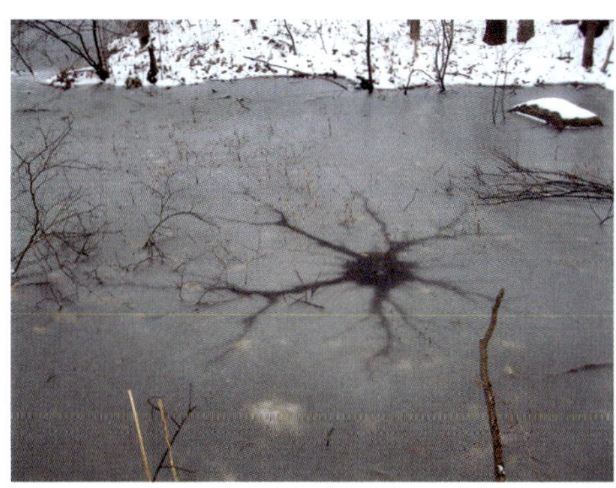

Ancestral Darkness

I come from hardy stock,
strong, adventuresome, intelligent—
but with brokenness woven in.
Ancestral darkness was always present.
I don't fully understand the many shards
of the despair and dysfunction
of previous generations,
and perhaps I never will.
But I always felt a nebulous, chilly energy—
an uneasiness that I couldn't explain.
It contained palpable sadness,
family relationships that had fallen by the wayside,
and a deeply entrenched code of silence.
This ancestral darkness does not define me,
but I grew up with the confusion and instability of its effects.
All along the way the Light of Love
illuminated my underpinnings when I needed it most,
but it was hard to relax in its warmth.
The resilience, courage, and perceptiveness
of my forbears were there, too.
So I've learned, adapted, expanded.
I am grateful, optimistic, grounded.
I am growing, healing, flowing.
I can trust in my abilities to care, communicate, connect,

and not worry about breaking the code.
It was theirs, not mine.
I can live in the Light,
be who I am.
It was there.
It was real.
But I don't have to live in the shadows
of ancestral darkness
anymore.

October 25, 2015

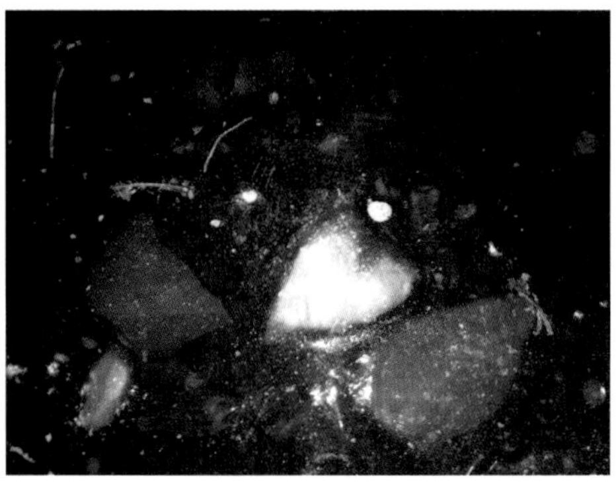

Your Presence

You show your presence in such
sweet subtleness.
Whether I'm unsure and questioning,
open and aware,
aching and weary,
or calmly experiencing me
in the newness of my life—
you are there.
Thank you, my love,
for helping me move ahead
with your gentle, consistent support.
In your absence I can still find
your presence,
and for that I am grateful.

January 24, 2016

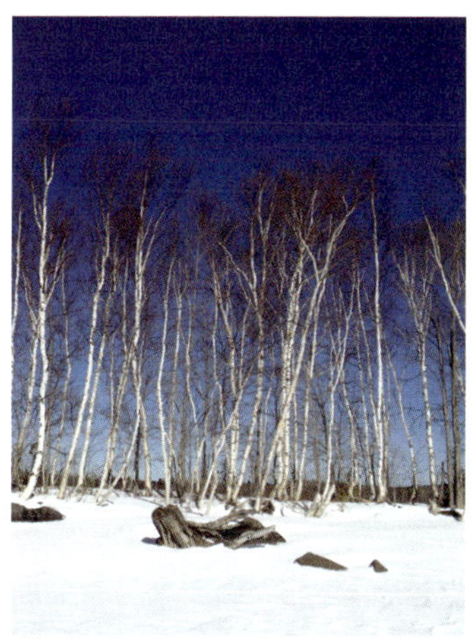

Enough

Separate and one
we stand strong by the shore
of a frozen windswept lake,
each of us rooted and whole.
Softly we sway as cool breezes
waft about us and we stretch
into a brilliant blue sky.
Majestic magical mountain range
watches over the valley scene
as stories are told,
new ones unfold,
and joy of togetherness binds.
Storm clouds may come another day,
and we'll weather whatever comes.
In this moment, however,
we have enough,
we are enough,
and we can simply be.

March 5, 2016

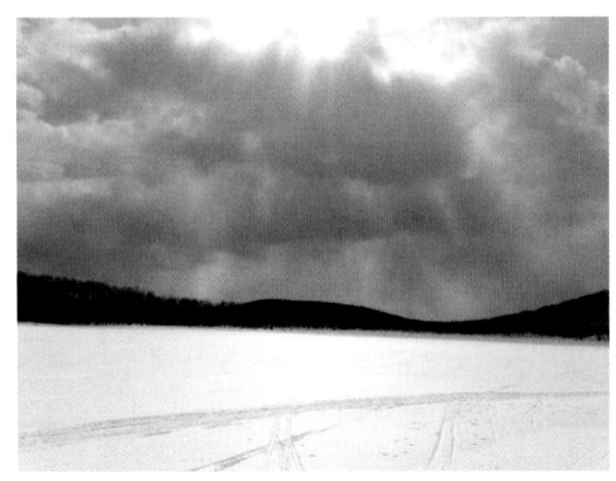

Let the Light Shine Through

Brilliant blues of the morning sky
become obscured by
shades of gray that
softly billow and swirl.
Winter sunbeams gently stretch
to frozen waters below.
As I continue to
learn and grow,
awaken and deepen,
I find I crave answers that
are definitive and clear.
I want those pristine blue skies
all around me,
to be free from any
residual, nebulous gloom.
When I discover that
what I thought I knew
is not entirely true
I adjust my path,
reorient my inner workings,
and stride ahead with gusto.
But, like benign clouds
above a snowy valley,
sometimes I just need
to slow down a bit and
let the light shine through.

March 13, 2016

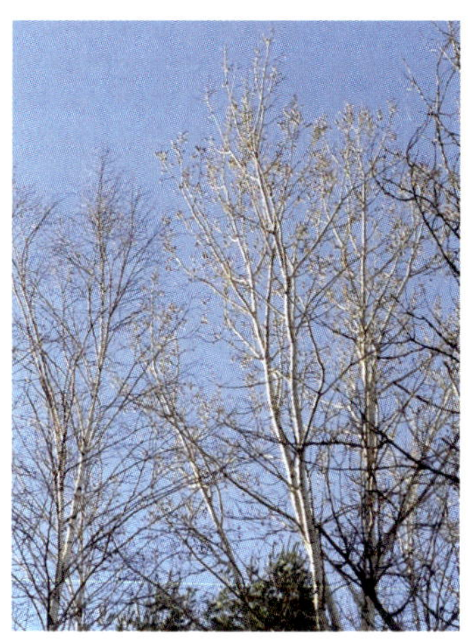

Morning Peace

Mellow morning sunlight
touches the tips
of budding trees,
washes down solid trunks
to the fertile ground.
Warmth invades
the coolness of night
as our nearest star
eases its way into the day.
Soft blue sky provides
a promising backdrop
to this gentle awakening
as chickadees chirp
their springtime song.
This being breathes deeply
as sensations of rootedness,
assimilation, and
expansion coexist.
Peace unfurling—
within and without.

April 20, 2016

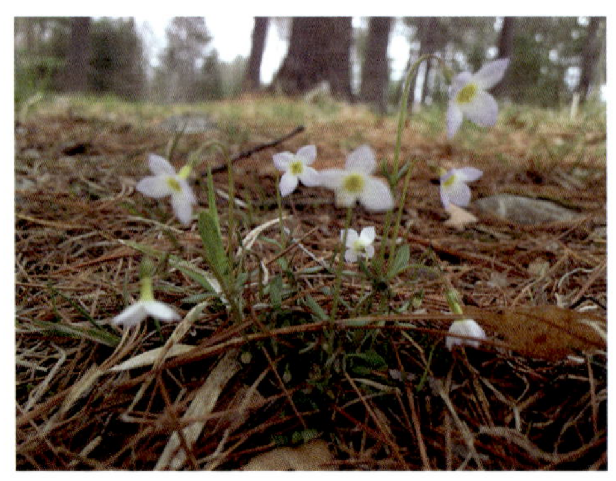

Filling In

Previously frozen ground
relaxes its hold and
vibrant growth arises.
Fertile soil fully awakens
under the coziness
of a spring sun.
Tender blossoms unfold
to share their quiet beauty,
basking in the light anew.
Prior growth
sustains this burgeoning
as chinks and breaches
near the roots replenish with
nourishment and flow.
No barriers now,
just a time to relish the releases,
treasure the tranquility,
and embrace the
filling in.

May 8, 2016

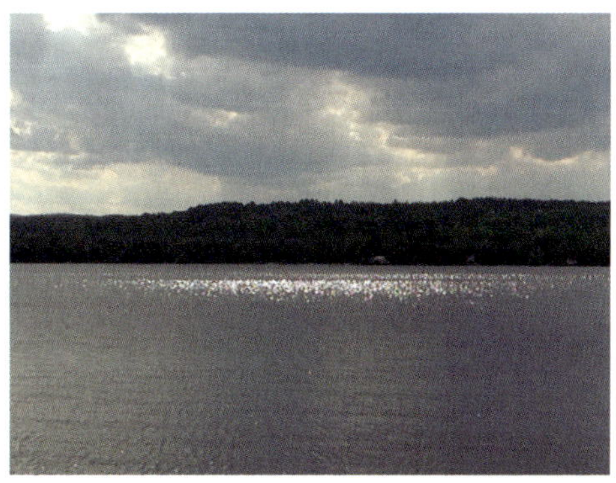

Sparkle Moments

Sparkle moments—
those times that
can quietly penetrate
the busy-ness of life.
How fortunate we are
that all around us
they dance.
Each of us a body
afloat on a tiny spinning
planet in the cosmos.
Our own entity
and part of a whole,
we need to pause and
allow the sparkle moments
to buoy us as we navigate
this intricate,
precious life.

July 7, 2016

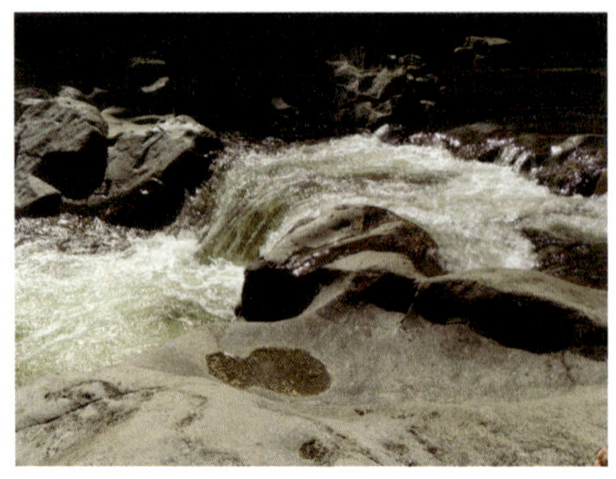

Let It Sing
(so I remember)

Drop in. Listen.
Allow the flow
from within.
Let the deep places speak—
from you, for you,
with you.
Notice what surfaces
as it swirls, sifts,
and then settles
just as you need
it to be.
In those moments
your heart sings a song
of you.
So drop in, listen,
and let it sing.

penned during a writing program with
Heather Sellers at Kripalu, August 1, 2016

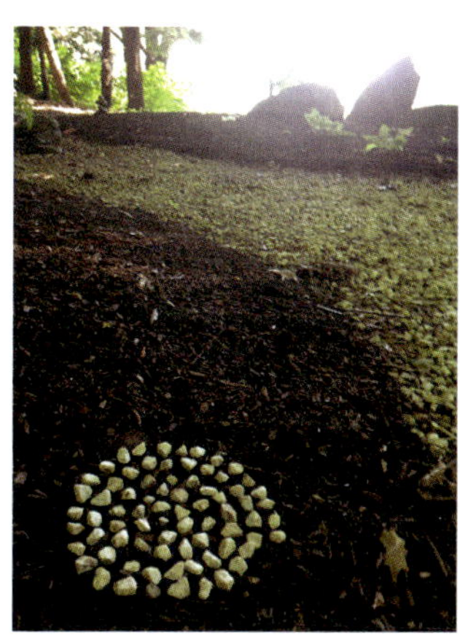

A Poem for Barry
(abecedarius)

A Poem for
Barry. May 29, 2002. I'm in my
classroom, but my attention is
drawn outward. Even sweet, second-grade
energy doesn't keep me fully
focused. A quiet, shy
girl asks for help. Two boys collaborate on 'The Anty Adventures of Bob and
Harry'. My ed tech talks with her
individual student as he works on a poem.
Jacob, my mathematician, writes his own
kind of story with numbers and words.
Light streams in the large casement windows,
making patterns on the worn hardwood floor.
No reason, but I walk
over, look out to see a Farmington
policeman stride toward the front door. I
quiver when the intercom beeps and I'm called down
right away. The
somber young officer tells me you collapsed playing
tennis, I'm needed at the hospital. Somehow I
understand that my life is shifting. The
very moment I turn into the hospital drive an energy
washes over me—strong, palpable, undeniable. Later I know
exactly what it is.
Your Love. I know this to be true. And like a
zephyr it weaves its way into my life, even today.

in my room at Kripalu, August 4 into 5, 2016

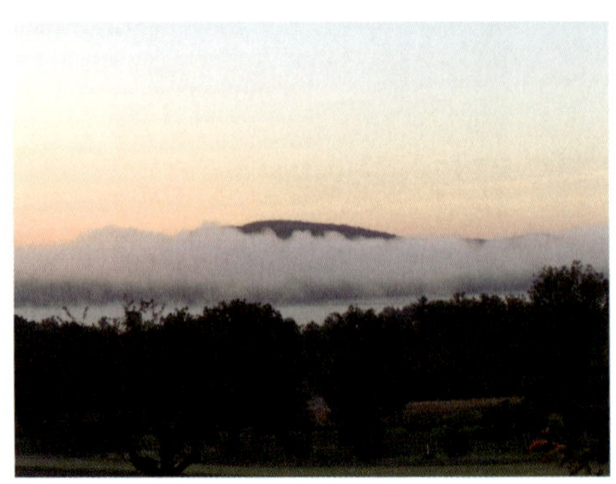

Softer Around Their Edges

Waters of being flow
with tender, tranquil freedom.
Still some spiral into depths,
re-emerge with fresh awareness.
Expanding currents of clarity wash away
stale doubts and fears
rooted in truths
that simply are not true.
Detached despair lifts, dissipates—
warmed by the light
of a brand new day.
Body twitches and quivers
with pristine energy
as bits and pieces settle,
softer around their edges
than ever before.

August 9, 2016

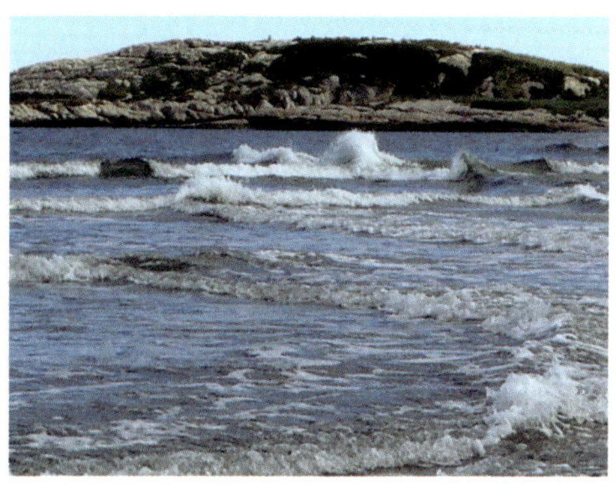

Cross-Currents

Strong, salty waves undulate with angst,
and the power of freedom.
Cross-currents collide,
entangle and rise,
sunlight illuminating
whatever surfaces.
Then the tides shift—
disentangle, release, reorganize,
and settle into a new flow.
Somewhere within the brine is me,
my authentic being.
When I am able to let go and
ride my unique currents
I am uncluttered, untethered,
unconfined.
My wonderful wild child glows,
her benevolent energy sparkling
with life.

September 24, 2016

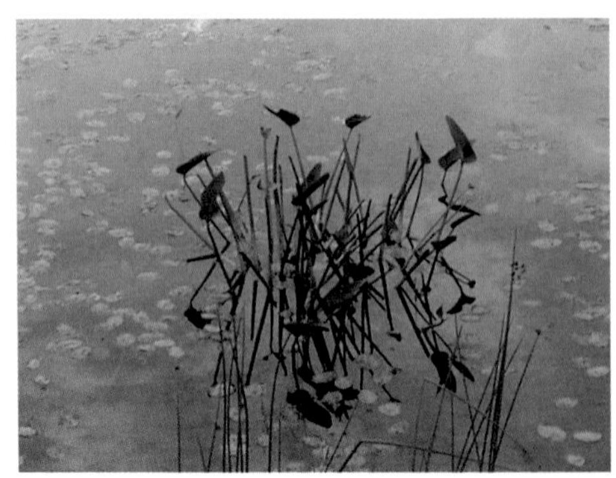

Stretching to Embrace

Rooted in divine fathoms,
my pristine pieces
stretch to embrace
the placid evening light.
Murky shadows,
not an accurate
reflection of my essence,
are simply part of my whole.
And I embrace them, too.
I can choose to befriend
all that has come before,
safe with the knowledge
that throughout my life
this benevolent spirit
has been fluid,
active and true.

September 25, 2016

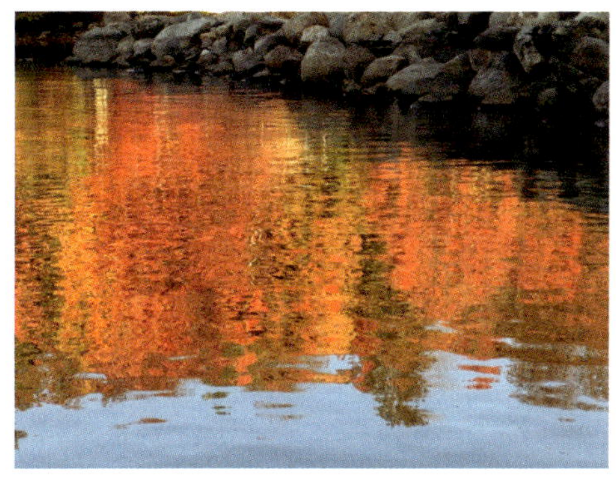

The Radiance of Change

As the currents of my being
become more fully free,
more often I have prolonged
moments of dropping into
my own validity.
Time and time again
congestion caused by
bygone perplexities unwinds
and allows for novelty
and liberation.
Rooted in rightness,
this involves a purposeful
willingness to let go.
I can't change what was,
only my reactions to what
is right in front of me.
Recognizing the possibility
of old patterns pulling me astray,
I can choose to rely upon
bedrock of excavated truths
to discover a new way through.
Lovingly, tenderly
I wrap my arms around
all I've been,
all I am,
and all I have left to be.
I encourage the freedom of unfettering,
nurture the power of presence, and
embrace the radiance of change.
There is beauty in me

right here, right now.
More and more I feel safe
to let it reflect and refract
into the light of day.

October 9, 2016

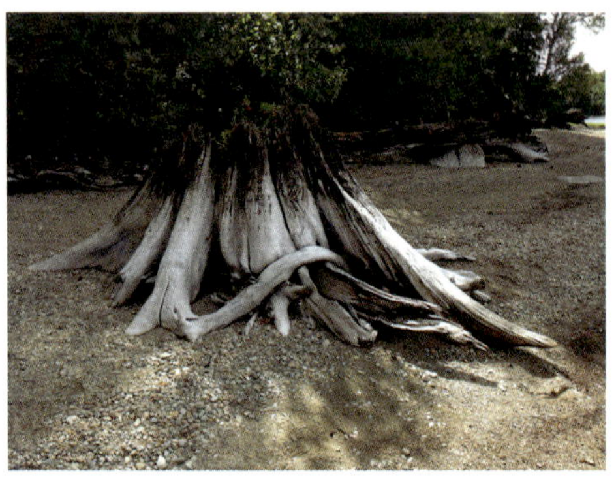

Rooted and Gentle Sadness

Here I am,
all these years since you died
on that heart-wrenching spring day,
and I miss you.
Though the ache is less potent,
I have a rooted and gentle sadness.
I'm so grateful that our lives came together
by the shores of Saddleback Lake,
that you had the patience to wait
for me to understand how
to accept your unconditional love.
I wish you could be standing with me,
hand in hand,
to witness our beautiful children
further widen into their lives,
with passions to follow
and loves of their own.
Sometimes I wonder if you
would know me now,
would love this rather different me.
And then I smile with the knowledge
that you knew all of me the whole time.

I do believe in the sensations of your presence,
in the radiance of change,
and in all the other understandings I've gleaned
through years of exploring
within and without.
But sometimes I just want your arms around me,
to feel the physical connection of your love,
to be together in the here and now.
This rooted and gentle sadness
is not wrong for me to feel.
I haven't failed at grieving.
It's just part of my shadows and,
in truth,
enhances my light.

October 10, 2016

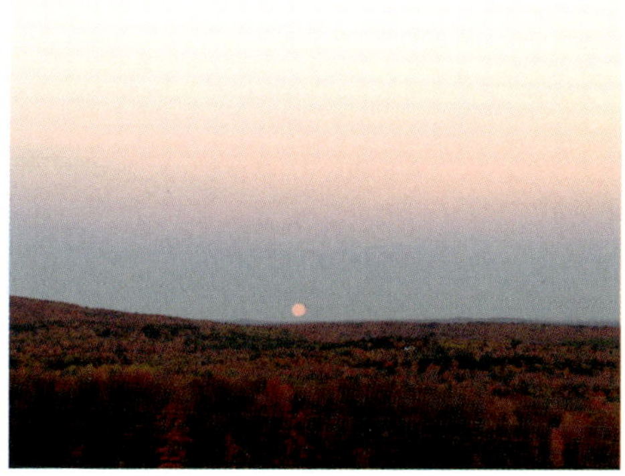

The Pull of the Moon

I sit alone atop
a gentle hill waiting,
believing that I'm looking
in the right direction.
My body aquiver with
the chill of the evening
and the excitement
of getting away,
I take some breaths—
deeper than
I've ever taken before.
I feel full

of me.
I settle some and
wonder when it will come.
Just then a sliver of
the pinkish orb
slides above the
multi-hued horizon
exactly where I'm looking.
I gasp a little
and then smile a
smile that I can feel
all through my body.
Slowly,
yet quickly,
the moon
continues its ascent
into the twilight sky.
I feel deeply grateful that
the pull of the moon
led me to be
right there,
right then,
just as I am.

October 16, 2016

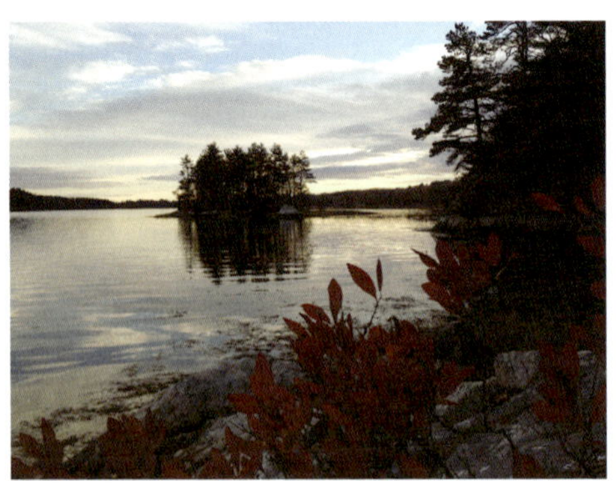

More Clearly Now

I can 'see' so much
more clearly now,
even through my tears.

Or more accurately,
because of them.
My body,
both an island
with clear boundaries
and an energetic entity
connected to all,
has forged the way
on this enlightening quest
to reveal truths in which
I can securely believe.
I am both awestruck
and humbled as
diverse treasures are
continually unearthed.
My inquiring mind still wonders
and worries a bit,
but when I relax into
my gentle, caring heart and
allow myself to linger,
exquisite multi-faceted
clarity eventually unfolds.
And sometimes I don't
really need to know,
simply to trust
in the spirit and
beauty of Love.
I have a sense of triumph
as I live in this world
more clearly now
as me.

November 6, 2016

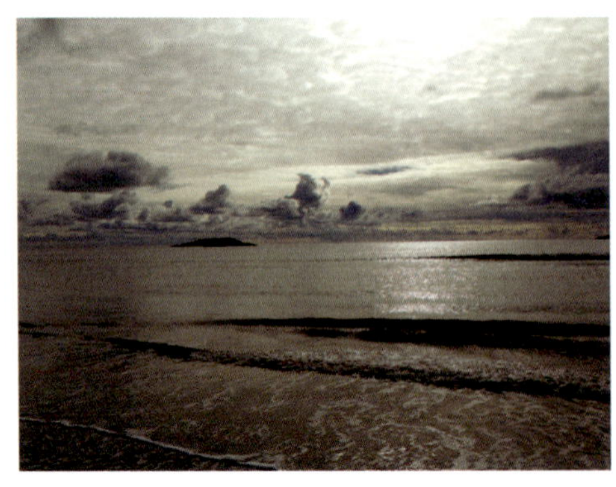

Just Stop

So much unease, discontent,
wonder and worry
coursing through our world.
One can easily be swallowed
by powerfully negative currents.
Strongly they pull,
pit us against one another,
make us judge and condemn—
if we succumb.
The future, as always, is uncertain.
It has become even more important to
just stop.
Look to the horizon to watch
multi-hued clouds
as they billow and blow,
to admire the dazzling colors of our
steady star as it rises and sets,
to behold the magic of the moon as it
travels our ever-present sky.
Listen to the sound
of ocean waves as they
softly break upon our solid shores,
to changing winds
as they make
naked trees dance,
to busy birds singing
their individual songs.
Pause to feel
grateful for the good things
in life,

to consider the thoughts
and feelings of those
with whom time is shared,
to simply be.
Be open to any opportunity
to soak in the positive currents
of the natural world,
of empathy and compassion,
of love shared.
Every so often
just stop—
look, listen, feel,
reset, be.

November 13, 2016

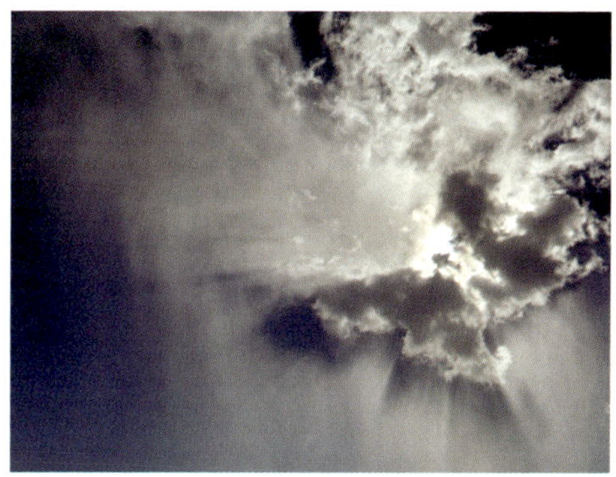

True Communion

Sensations of ease allow
my body to move
more freely
despite minor limitations of
age-old injuries.
A slight need to reach, do,
continues to lessen as
billowing love spreads to the
boundaries of my being.
Sometimes … all at once breathless, but not.
More like a suspension of breath,
a pause for moments of
transition and stillness,

then somehow breathing anew.
A gentle sense of being adrift,
but not off course,
as I restart, reset, reconnect.
On my own two feet,
yet held and supported.
The way it should be,
should have been
all along.
Various eras of my life blend together
as I stretch into the fullness
of my substance.
Doubts and fears rooted in bygone days
come to the surface of my mind,
begging to still be heard.
But it's in my power to turn away,
and to.
There's more, beyond my knowing.
Nothing to do but
allow healing to absorb,
have faith in
true communion,
and be me.

December 28, 2016

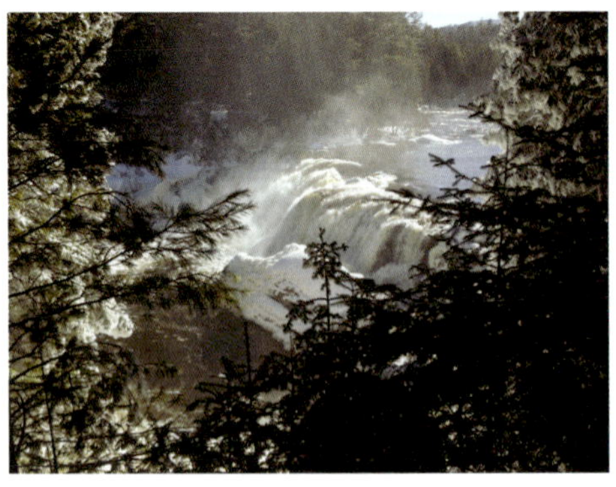

Watery Wisdom

Varied currents within
a body whole,
ranging from

grief to gratitude,
fear to joy,
despair to faith.
Transitory emotions that
ebb and flow within us all,
a true human experience.
Jagged, frozen places
can and will thaw
in the right way,
at the right time,
if one makes the choice
to dive in and explore
the depths of being.
A drip or two at a time
may join the stream,
or an opening may form
whitewater wildness
with an energy of its own.
When the times are right
the vapors of angst will release,
allowing for moments of stillness,
chances to explore eddies
as they swirl and adjust,
or simply the opportunity
to let go,
let flow.
The one constant in life
is change,
as reflective,
bubbling,
trickling,
streaming,
cascading
waters
so clearly
show.
Water knows,
and deep inside
we do, too.

March 12, 2017

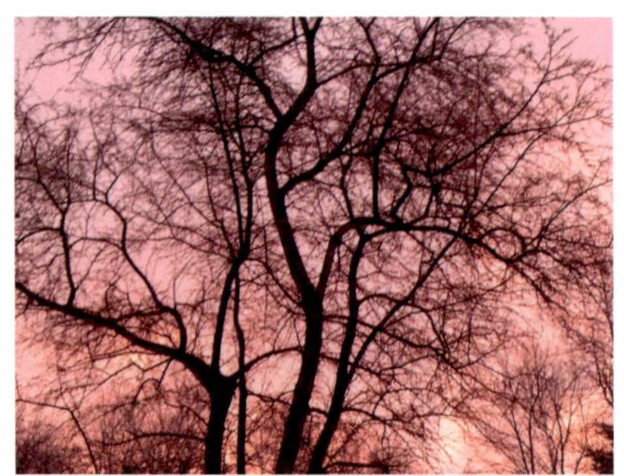

Mourning Light

No one has the right
to tell another where
or when or how
to grieve.
A softness comes
to mourning
as authentic
emotions are free
to come to light.
A gentle dawning unfolds,
surrounds,
weaves its way
within and without,
a welcome glow of
ethereal awareness.
As morning sun penetrates
the darkness of night,
so does mourning light
seep its way into
a being who chooses
to explore the
diverse and intricate
facets of grief.
What a pure and
tender experience
it is to behold
and embrace
the beauty,
the grace,

the rightness
of mourning light.

March 23, 2017

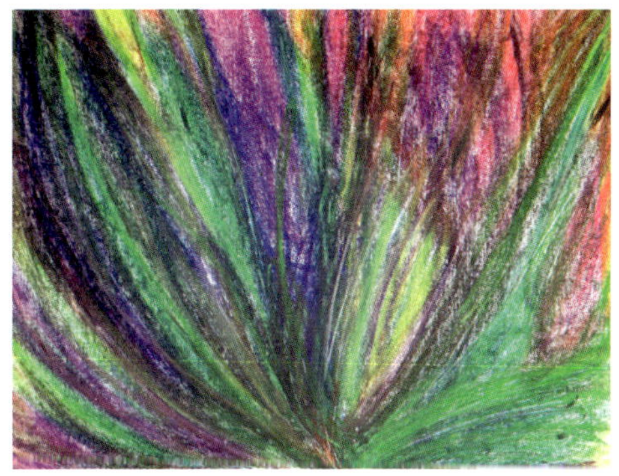

Mother Love

I open sleepy eyes and see her
peering over the edge of the crib,
carefully checking … on me.
The pureness of her
love oozes over the rail,
between the slats
as it gently winds around
and through my being.
Her kind eyes sparkle with the
simple joy of being my mom.
I feel comfortable
within though
my blanket has fallen away,
the warmth of her guardianship
and acceptance
wrapping me in safety.
She picks up my blanket,
folds it and sets it aside.
She knows that in that moment
I have no need for it.
Slowly and gently she slides
her hands under me and lifts.
I am at once suspended
and connected,

my foundation
healthy and strong.
She lays me against her and
I feel our hearts beating together,
though each has a chest of its own.
I snuggle my face
into the tenderness of her skin,
close my eyes and
allow myself to soak in
the sweet, soft sensations of
Mother Love.

April 4, 2017

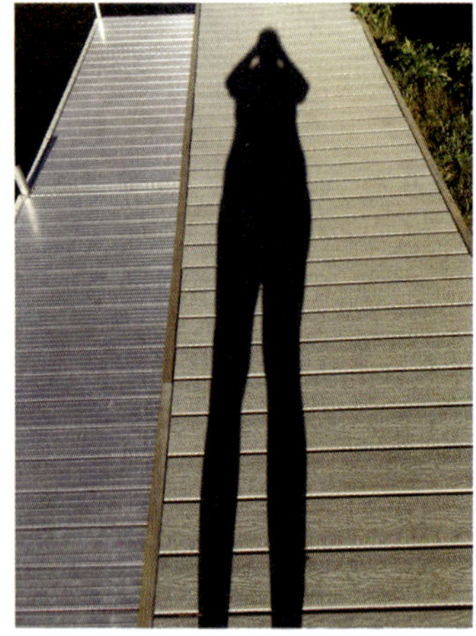

This Body

This body is mine to inhabit.
In this dwelling I am safe.
I am free.

There were times in my younger days
that were fearsome and confusing
to one who was caring, vulnerable, trusting.
Some of the details are clear,
some escape me.
But I know that I felt threatened,
that I was stifled and hurt
along the way.

Deep within parts of me went cold
as a way to protect.
The love that was present
often became tainted by
anger and disdain that were not mine,
though I thought were because of me.
I now know that is false,
but for a very long time
it felt true.

The truth is that I have a warm and caring heart.
I have lived my life from a place of compassion,
even in the midst of the chaos that sometimes ensued.
I knew to trust in the mutual love
of a soulmate who came into my life
exactly when we needed each other.
I have a mind that craves understanding,
finds meaning,
and is learning to accept quiet,
that it doesn't have to work so hard all the time.
I have a sweet, sensitive soul
that is less and less encumbered
by the lingering constraints
of those dismal, baffling times.
I recognize and can accept the power of Love
with the realization that I don't only have to give,
it is safe and right to also receive.
Body, mind and spirit—
expanding, healing, thriving
together within.

This body is mine to inhabit.
In this dwelling I am safe.
I am free.

April 9, 2017

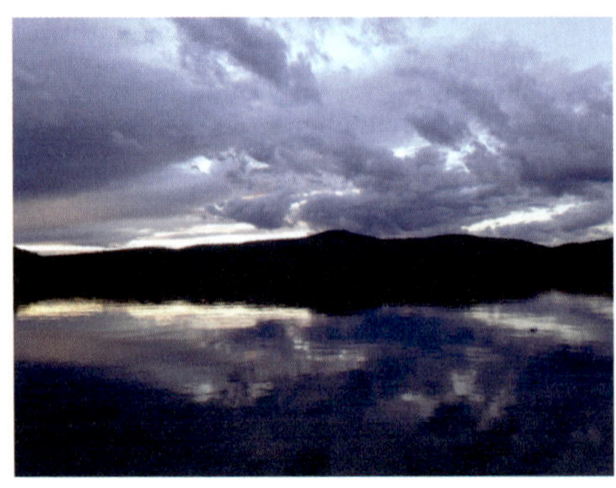

Father Love

Gentle, steady acceptance
coupled with a deep, strong sureness.
I know you've been there all along,
but for varied reasons I just couldn't
quite trust all the way, all the time.
I thought I had to hide, protect,
stay strong on my own.
But, just when I was beginning to
understand the primary reasons
for perceived wrongness,
there you were.
In those sweet, tender moments
between sleep and awakening,
you simply sat with me in silence
until I became aware of your presence.
One hand on my shoulder, one on my leg,
you calmly offered compassionate connection
without judgment.
I didn't even ask you to come,
at least not to my knowledge,
so your visit was a pleasant surprise.
I vacillated between
communion and old patterns of unease.
Even now, though,
I can remember the energy of sitting with you
and how it felt benevolent and right.
No reason to fear, no need to be ashamed
or feel anything but love.
After letting those sensations
sit and settle for a while

I realize what you offered that morning
was unconditional Father Love—
that, in truth, it's always there.
It's reminiscent of moments
with my dad, learning the stars
and finding pictures in the clouds,
of what I saw in my brother's eyes
as he watched his babies for too few years,
and what I felt with Barry as we reveled in being
with our babies, children, young adults.
I miss them all so very much—
dad, brother, husband.
I know their love is with me still,
as I'm becoming more free
to receive, embrace your love.
Perhaps it is actually all the same force.
Thank you for your visit
in the wee hours of the morning
to help me be more aware,
more accepting of ubiquitous
Father Love.

May 16, 2017

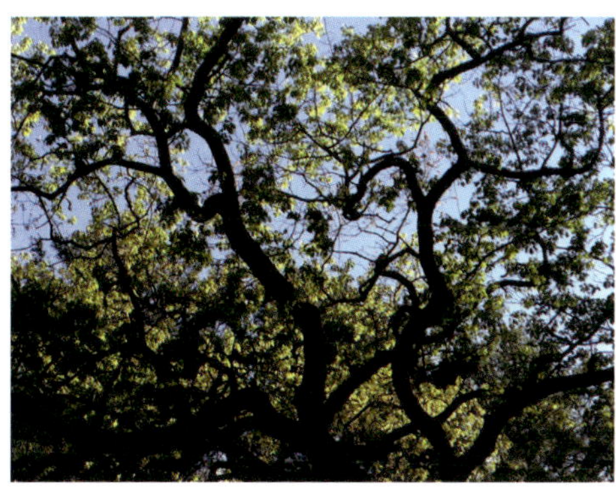

Peaceful Acceptance

Tender moments of connection
await awareness as
the need for understanding relaxes.
Simultaneously sinking in and rising up,
one is able to

access knowing,
trust togetherness,
savor the freshness
and energy of expansion.
Waters of being flow freely,
breath diffuses deeply,
heart pulsates purely,
and there is a tuning in,
a tuning out.
Bits of bedrock beneath
may rumble or tumble,
then sift and settle
in new places
with a sweet sense
of realignment,
a suspension of striving,
an opportunity to just be.
Tangled tendrils
no longer matter
and the taproot is nourished
by what is real and right,
as it has been all along.
A reaching without seeking,
a simple stretching,
a peaceful acceptance of now.

May 21, 2017

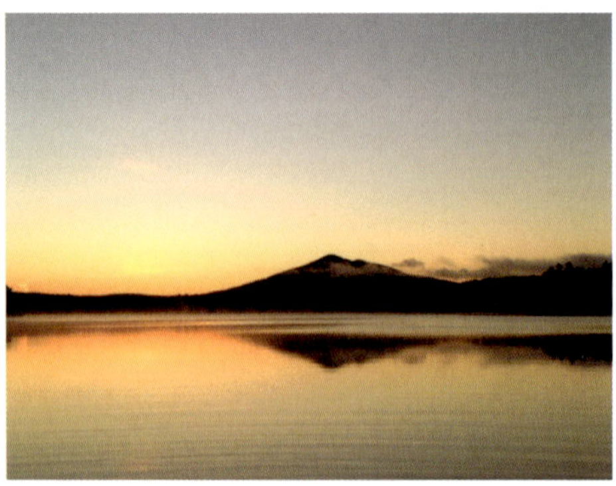

Cozy Light

In awakening there is a recognition of arrival
coupled with departure,

in the ongoing progression of time.
A subtle lightening as newness slowly unfolds,
bringing with it familiarity
and the unknown.
All that has been is present,
like a solid mountain silhouetted
against a fledgling sky,
calmly reflected in the fluid depths.
Some of what was will wash away,
carried by currents of watery wisdom.
Movement that is understood,
or not.
Quiet clouds may
work their way into the scene,
flowing with the winds,
be they gentle or strong.
All that will be is yet to come
as the softness of the rising sun widens
and stretches into the light of day,
the hopeful promise of clear skies
ever present and real.
Solitary being surveys the scene,
ponders and wonders,
then draws in her breath,
grateful for the moment she is in.
She feels a sense of immersion,
as a freedom unlike
any she has ever known gradually unfurls.
She kindles her inner embers
to let the cozy light of newness
permeate her body
and expand out into the developing day,
willing any remaining debris
to softly flow away.

May 30, 2017

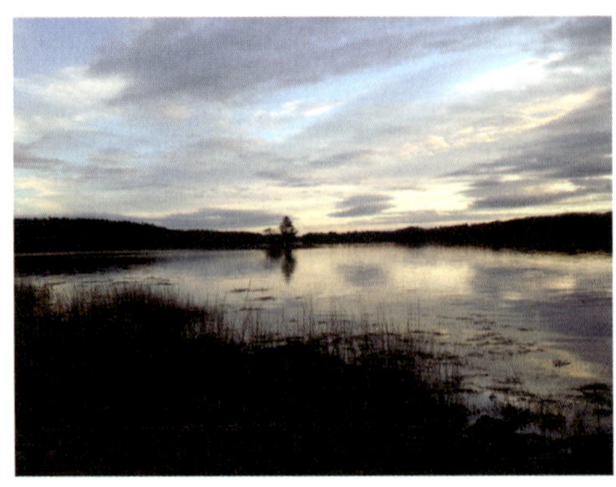

Sweet Safety

Peaceful, restorative energy widens,
oozing into once-hidden spaces.
Unbidden,
it simply flows wherever
there is a need.
Kind-hearted, loving being
knows now to simply allow
and welcome,
without worry or defense.
More to do, more to grow,
more to heal—
but, in those moments
she settles in to the sensations,
relishes the revelations,
honors her health.
She recognizes and embraces
the sweet safety that
should have been hers all along,
and is deeply grateful for
its expansion
into her everyday life.

August 15, 2017

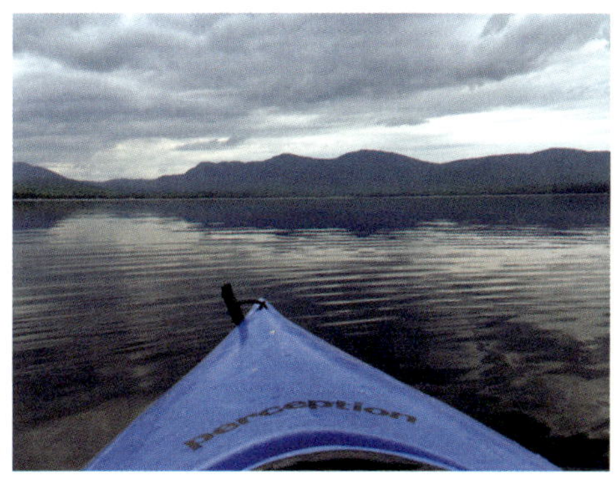

Finding Our Way Home

I've been traveling for a while now,
searching for something
I couldn't fully define,
at least in my little girl world.
She grew and thrived
despite this missing link.
Together we found Love
and have accessed healing,
but we still remained unsure.
That beautiful little girl,
now held and honored by me,
was never comfortably
at home before.
We've discovered that
what we've been looking for
truly is within and without,
has been all along.
It's safe to believe
and it's right to let go.
As we do that we are
heartfully, soulfully, lovingly
finding our way home
to our place of peace,
to the sanctity of self.

September 12, 2017

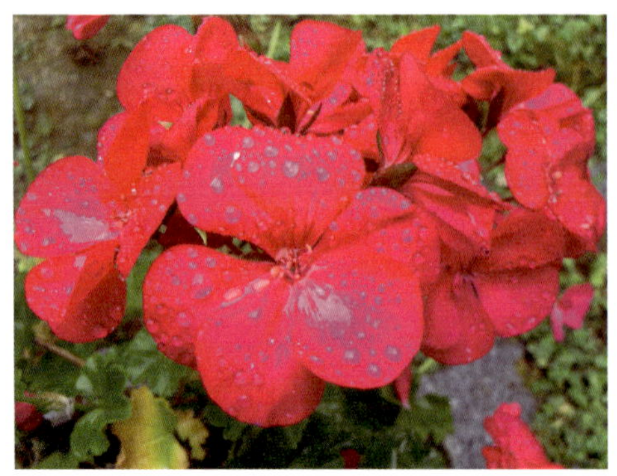

It's Done

It's done, sweet Sarah.
All over, finished—
and we survived.
Actually, we did much more than that.
Despite the weight of the
layers of pain and fear,
we learned and loved,
wondered and wandered,
giggled and grew.
We thrived.
It's time to embrace the fact
that you are not wrong, have never been.
Those scary experiences were real.
They did happen,
but not because of anything you did.
Nothing from those bygone days
can get you now.
What is true is that you are good,
I am good,
and together we can let
that part of our lives be over.
It's done,
but we most definitely are not.
I am so excited to see what will come
as, together, we continue
to relax and let that big, bold energy
show its beautiful blossoms
as they stretch out into the light of day.
I will tenderly nurture all they contain
and let them show their true colors.

The sacred connection between
adult and child is right here within.
The sacred connection with whatever
you feel comfortable calling the Divine
is right where it has always been—
available, steady, real.
It's safe, it's right, it's time
to trust in both
because it's done.

October 12, 2017

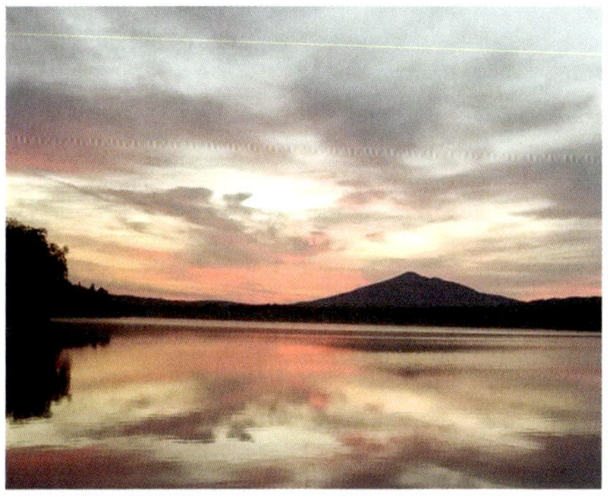

Sweet Safety, Deepened

When I slow down, take a pause,
I become more fully acquainted
with the tender, loving support
of the Divine.
Once a fledgling at this,
more and more I am able to
let myself relax into it
without reservation.
As I do,
my appreciation
of its bounty and benevolence
strengthens.
I thought I already had this, knew this,
but the beautiful reality of healing
is that, once invited,
it happens in its own time,
doesn't need to be forced,

or judged.
The more one settles,
the more there is to discover.
There are moments
when this deep healing feels like
a viscous, balmy tonic
with an amazing propensity
of seeping into the spaces
and places that need it most.
It caresses and coats them,
sinking to the depths
like the fine sediment of
gently flowing water.
Particles of past traumas
swirl away with the flow,
and there is visceral relief
as that sense
of sweet safety
deepens.

November 11, 2017

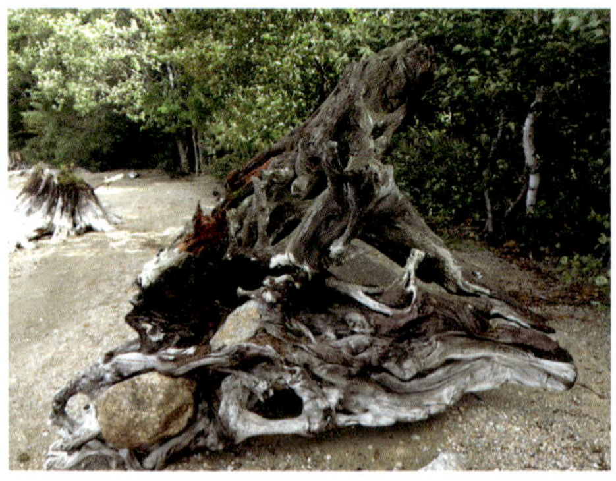

Push Away

Push away, push away,
powerful arms hold me at bay.
Then—come in, give me advice,
help me know how to be.
I tried so hard to do what was asked,
my young mind trained to be adept
at searching for answers

that were not mine to find.
Yet, even when I did,
the push-away happened,
again and again.
My being became used to
this pull and this push,
mostly the push.
Then he came along,
gently invited me all the way in.
With great patience and care
he let me know that I was welcome
just as I was,
that his arms were loving and safe.
It felt so good to belong.
Through the struggles that life
inevitably contains,
our union was strong and sure.
When he died it made sense
that I felt lost and undone.
Now, all these years later,
one of the many things
I recognize is that
my early experiences
had me believing
that God was pushing me away, too.
That was real for me,
and yet not true.
Those fierce arms
of rejection and disapproval
have lost most of their power.
I can appreciate my actual foundation,
relish the knowledge
that it's been there all along.
As imposed falseness crumbles away,
I carefully, steadily
allow myself to believe
that God's arms are loving and safe, too.

November 23, 2017, Thanksgiving

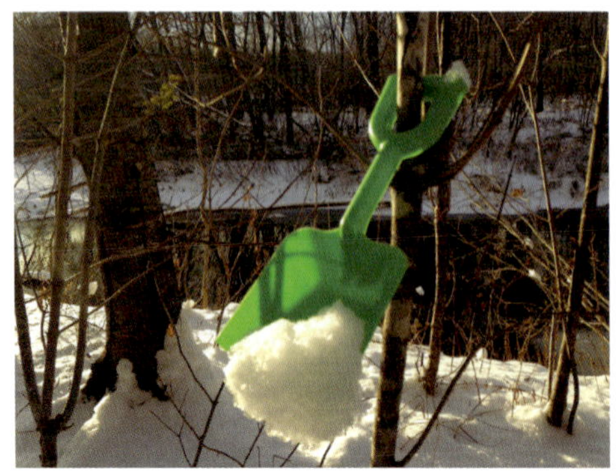

Make No Mistake

I recently realized
that I've lived just about all of my life
trying to not make any mistakes.
The definition of a mistake was nebulous,
didn't come from me,
involved fear and threat.
This has been quite a revelation.
I mean, really?
I spend all my working days teaching children
that it's okay to stumble,
that those are the times when we learn the most.
They know I accept them right where they are,
will stand by them as they recover from a blunder,
will walk with them as they move ahead.
And, in truth,
I have lived that
on some level within, as well.
But way, way, way deep down inside
the drive to make no mistake
has been a strong and swift undercurrent
with a surreptitious potency.
It made me quick to accept responsibility
whenever anything went wrong.
For so very long I assumed that the
'push aways' were always totally my fault.
I had this weird double standard
where I understood other people's
struggles so easily and could
be there to support and help.
Yet, mine were because

I must have made a mistake
somewhere along the way
and I deserved to hurt.
Make no mistake?
Humanly impossible!
And so now I must remember to
be gentle with my self
as I recover and move ahead.
I will gratefully continue to receive,
allow caring and healing
to dilute and diffuse,
as the burdens I lugged for so long
continue to slip away.
Message to self:
make no mistake—
I am perfectly human,
just like anyone else.

December 12, 2017

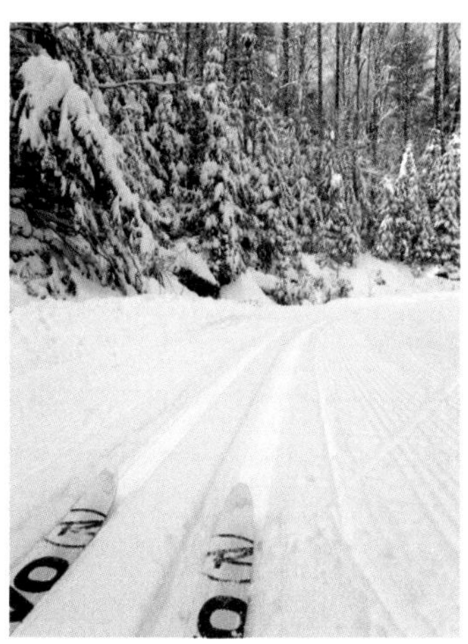

On the Right Track

Oftentimes I do feel
I am on the right track.
I attend to my valid sorrows,
welcome breathy joys,
value my unique self.
I am full of purpose,

radiance, and vitality.
But then sometimes
I feel adrift, lonely,
and weary of grief.
Today tears surfaced and
I couldn't identify their origin.
They came quickly,
caught me by surprise,
clearly needed to flow.
They came and they went,
but left me with a gentle unease.
I believe that some
of the defunct lessons
I absorbed are still
unsnarling and
I don't need to understand
the leftover tangles.
Just the writing of that
produces peace.
I can feel my body relax,
my mind settle,
my spirit soothe.
I think I will make the choice
to gratefully and lovingly
continue on my way,
trust that I truly am
on the right track.

December 27, 2017

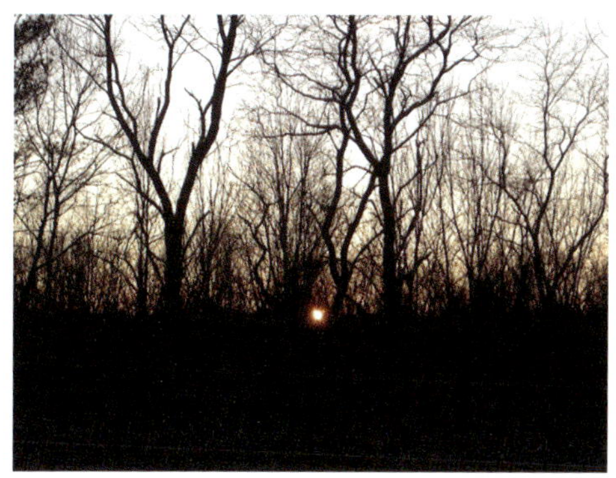

Solstice Sun

Solstice sun slips behind
a familiar landscape
and the darkest day is done.
That sun, though visible for so little time,
still holds warmth and brightness.
In truth, it's us here on Earth who
are in cyclical motion,
but we perceive the sun
as traversing across our sky.
The Solstice sun rides low on the horizon,
casts long shadows,
helps us recognize
the impact of the dark.
For many days onward
there is a lightening as
radiance expands in a
rather imperceptible way.
This lightening brings with it
a deeper warmth,
a crystallizing of hope,
the promise of new life to come.
Surely the dark is part of the cycle,
will always be,
but if one is aware and
notices the expansion,
there is further opportunity
to open to the possibilities
that accompany the
splendor of light.

December 28, 2017

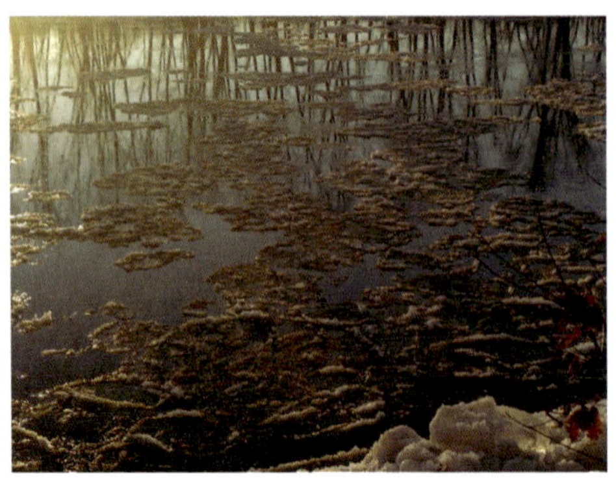

Ice Whispers

Deep freeze,
lasting for so very long.
And then … a thaw,
with torrential rains
and howling winds,
that lifts waters,
cracks layers of ice,
sets great chunks free.
Almost to flood level,
the river rushes through the valley
carrying the ice
until great pieces
pile upon one another
in a jumble.
Rains continue,
then subside,
allowing waters
to settle and recede.
Little by little
chunks release,
soften in milder temperatures
and the warmth of the sun.
Gently, more gently
the river flows.
Slushy pillows of
residual ice glide,
bump gently into each other
as they ride along.
Merging and diverging,
they whisper of

wisdom gleaned
from the freezing,
the flooding,
and the freeing.

January 15, 2018

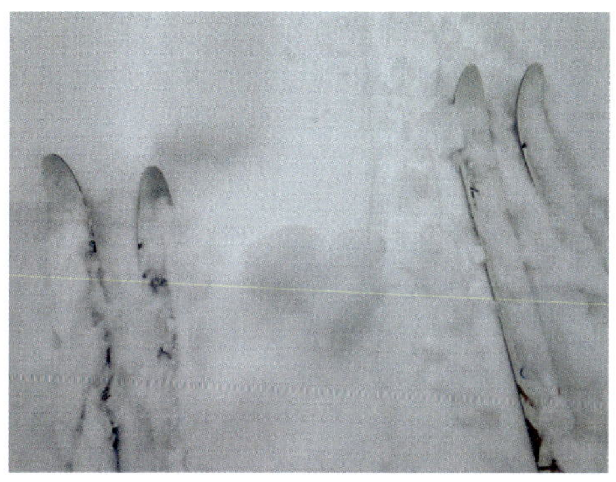

Soft-Hearted

Silently their skis glide along
a packed trail
that meanders through
the piney woods.
Trunks, branches, and boughs
cradle the still-sparkling snow
deposited by an earlier storm.
Emerging from the trees
onto a frozen pond
they marvel at the stillness
of the winter scene.
Climbing temperatures cause
low clouds to cling
to the surrounding hills,
enhancing their sense of serenity.
Tracks of varied woodland creatures
criss-cross the trail they follow,
the sense of adventure strong within.
Pausing for conversation they
notice a snowy heart right in
middle of their path.
Soft-hearted beings, both,

they share cozy moments
of understanding, friendship,
and awe.
The one writing these words
connects ever more deeply
to the tenderness of her
healing heart.

February 11, 2018

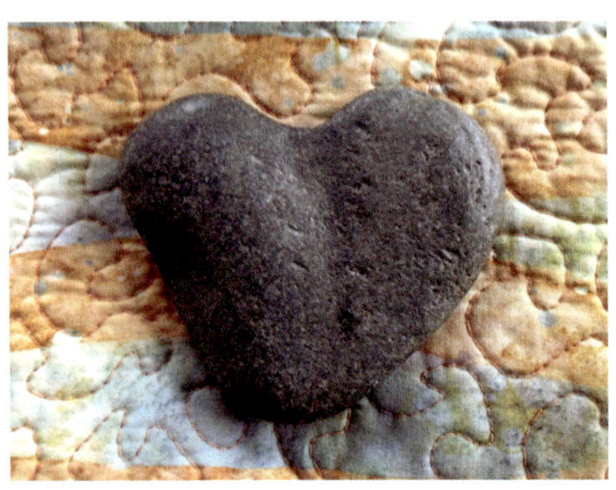

I'm Already Armed

I am a teacher
and I'm already armed.
My ammo consists of
empathy, kindness, passion,
hope, and concern.
My clip includes a deep desire
for my students to grow and learn
as much as they can while they
are in my care.
And care for them, I do.
Each and every day I welcome them
with open arms,
and together
we attack fractions, grammar,
scientific discovery, social constructs,
long division, informational writing,
reading comprehension strategies,
and so much more.
I strive to equip my students

with tools for life
like mindfulness, heartfulness,
creativity, self-expression,
and belief in their individual worth.
The only call to arms I would accept
is to embrace
my school community
even more.
Such are the arms
that the children of our world
yearn for and deserve.
Caring, connected arms
that hold on and let go
at the very same time.
Arms that support and accept,
encourage expansion
and promote peace.
These are the arms that
belong in schools.
I am a teacher
and I'm already armed.

February 23, 2018

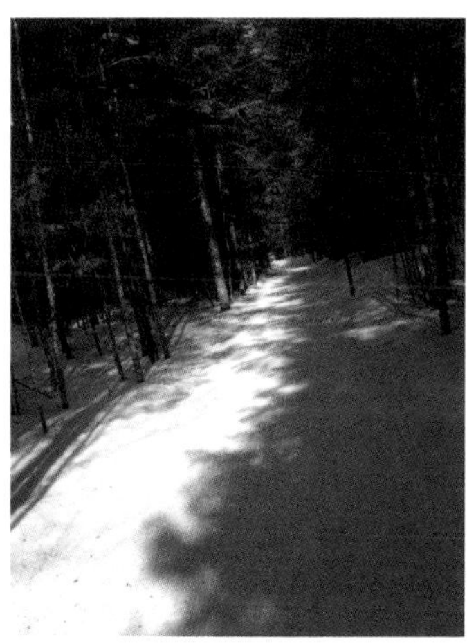

Here I Am

Liberated little one—
brimming with wants and needs,
joy and wonder,

curiosity and concern,
hope and love.
Smiles and frowns come more freely
as our integral being
relaxes into now.
Energies combine
into a fervent, flowy mix
as the effects of a turbulent past
continue to diminish and disperse.
Sorrows such as the
long-ago loss of a brother
may be felt anew,
as stifled emotions
are allowed and honored.
Triumphs such as the
birth of a brand new book
are safe to embrace,
as our words of healing are
heartfelt and genuine.
Like sunbeams and shadows
on a deep woods trail,
the interplay creates
a pleasant, intricate whole.
We can rest easy in the moment,
savor our vitality,
appreciate our place
within the vastness
of it all.
We can simply say,
"Here I am, this is me,"
and see where next
the open pathways may lead.

March 8, 2018

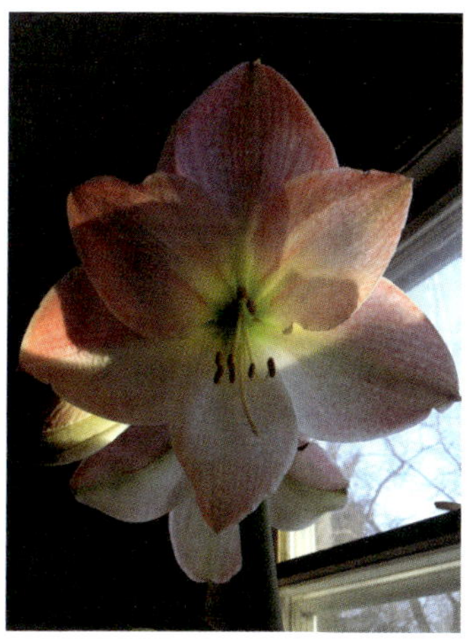

Sweet Relief

Wide open, full-on feeling,
wholly being in the body.
No threat to allowing
the full spectrum of emotions
that accompany being human.
They come, go, ebb, flow
with absolutely no need to feel wrong.
Even the sense of teetering on the edge
of previous pitfalls,
maybe even slipping in a bit,
carries no danger.
Remembering to ponder, consider,
determine what is truly going on
within and without.
Simply sitting with the
sensations and emotions,
letting the truth unroll, caress, and protect
like a warm, wooly blanket.
No concern of being 'too' of anything—
quiet, loud, happy, sad,
weak, strong, energetic, weary.
What sweet relief all this exploring
is bringing to this wide-eyed warrior.
Intrepid, soft-hearted, loving spirit
joyfully embraces the solace
that more and more saturates her cells.
Sweet, gentle, loving relief

with moments of no hurt,
no worries, no wonders,
and no threat … even to that.

March 20, 2018

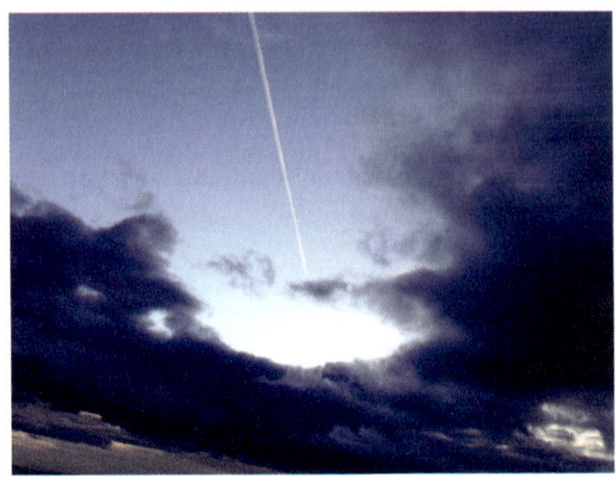

Godwink

Softly, subtly,
sometimes sidled with
stale achiness,
pieces rearrange, find newness
within her sweet, solid structure.
Now and then mild confusion
accompanies this realignment.
She simply notices,
acknowledges,
turns to faith.
She's ready and willing
to allow and accept this
as she knows her existence
is true.
Profound moments of
sublime serendipity
present themselves along the way.
She knows to immerse,
let them soak into her being,
cleanse and aid in healing.
Pensive, tender face of a young boy
as he shares a deep sorrow and his
own moments of healing.

Joyful energy of adult offspring
swooping down the slopes
of a beloved mountain.
Depth of sensitivity as a blind friend
raises his voice in song, adding to
the beauty of an Easter sunrise
on that same mountain.
Perfect punctuation of that celebration
as a contrail is lit by the rising sun,
dark clouds parting.
Not-so-random conversation
with a genial couple celebrating
an anniversary,
speaking of love and connection,
children now grown,
teaching and learning,
and the birth of a book.
"We're all supposed to be here
right now," says the woman.
"This is a Godwink."
This poet quietly smiles
and agrees.

April 3, 2018

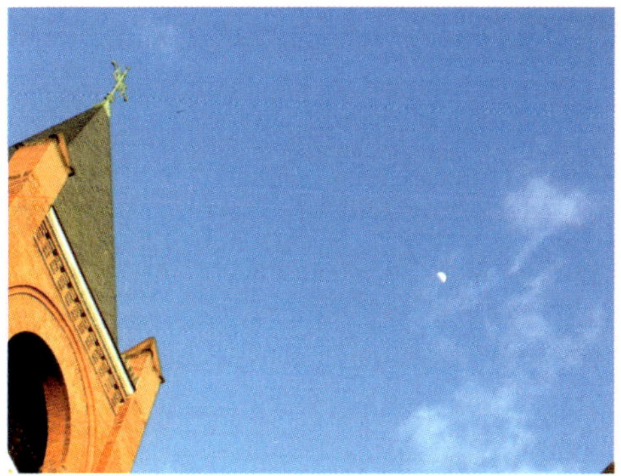

Right to Doubt

Imposing man in long white robes
compels somber people
to kneel, stand, speak, sing,
be quiet.

No apparent rhyme or reason
to the messages,
as they all seem based in threat.
Every so often he comes out
from behind what keeps him separate
and swings a smoky, smelly canister.
Rosy-cheeked girl
holds a hymnal in her gloved hand,
swings her Mary Jane-clad feet
as she looks, listens, smells,
strains to understand.
Despite her efforts,
she only fully takes in fear.
"Why?" she wonders.
"Don't they see, hear,
feel the truth?"
Her little stomach churns
as she squirms in the pew.
Years pass
and still she wonders, fears.
But she instinctively also
knows to embrace the good and,
as a young adult,
she finds unconditional love.
Together they thrive,
through thick and thin.
And then, one day he is gone.
Broken-hearted, she carries on—
eventually heeds the tug,
embarks on a journey within.
Her trek is long and arduous,
though much is discovered along the way.
She's grateful she knew to take the plunge.
She finds places of flowing,
of growing and knowing,
on which she is continually
learning to rely.
She cuddles her little one,
who had every right to doubt
the missives of that scary place.
As time goes on she is
better able to rest easy,
digest the awareness that

it's right to release,
right to trust,
right to commune,
right to
not feel wrong.

April 7, 2018

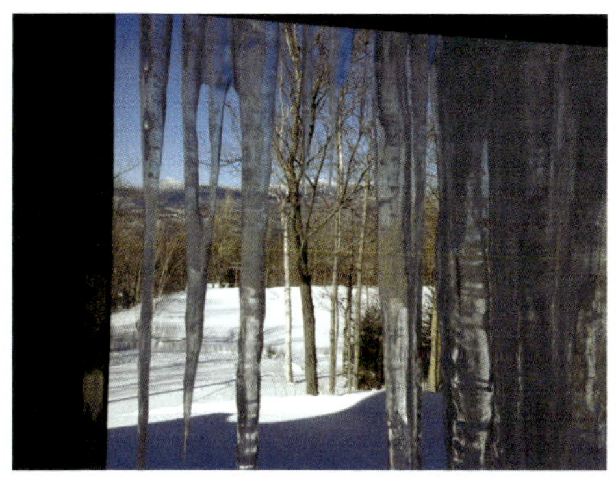

Heartened

(Take Away the T and move the R)

Threatened.
That's what I felt for much
of my life.
Not just fear, but threat—
here, there, everywhere,
ready to pounce at any opportunity.
It had long been lurking,
creeping around the deep recesses of me,
keeping some parts of me captive.
In my healing I have gleaned some
understanding of the varied reasons
as to why and how that happened.
I know those multiple causes
were anchored to diverse stanchions.
As my mind has opened to
novel ways of thinking,
my heart to new ways of feeling,
my spirit to unique ways of expanding,
I can see and feel that,
in truth,

I should be heartened
by what I have accomplished,
how I have lived.
I can safely honor
my generosity, wit, and resilience.
So I think I'll just
take away the t and move the r,
change feeling threatened
to being heartened
in the multi-hued,
softened moments of the
here and now.

April 11, 2018

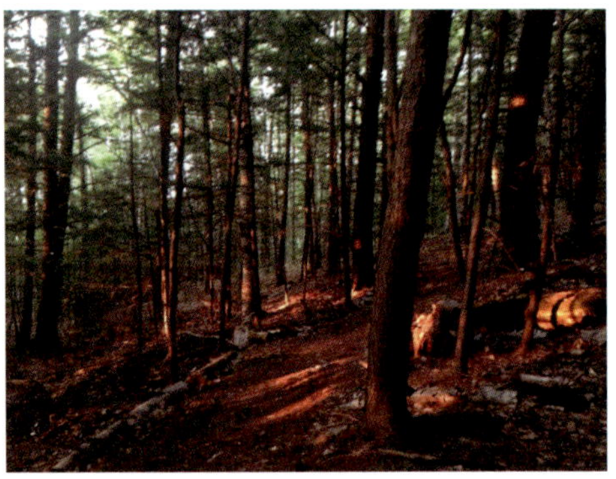

Go There

Don't go there—
worst advice ever.
At least it was for me.
In truth,
it became vital to go into
that which was causing my dis-ease.
You can wrap it up,
store it away,
deny its existence.
But *there* IS there,
will continue to be.
It's not easy to take the leap,
plunge on in.
It can't really be done alone,

so you'll have to ask for help.
You'll need support and love,
but when the time is right,
when you hear the call or
feel the tug,
go there.
You'll learn and grow,
gather what is necessary,
enabling you to take
what *there* has to teach
and utilize it for good.
Over time you will discover
slivers of understanding,
shards of insight,
specks of wisdom
that, together,
provide illumination and peace.
There has virtues all its own
that will mingle and mesh with
here and now,
revealing the beauty
of a familiar landscape
anew.
So *go there*—
wander and wonder,
explore and examine,
and in time,
restore and recover.

April 24, 2018

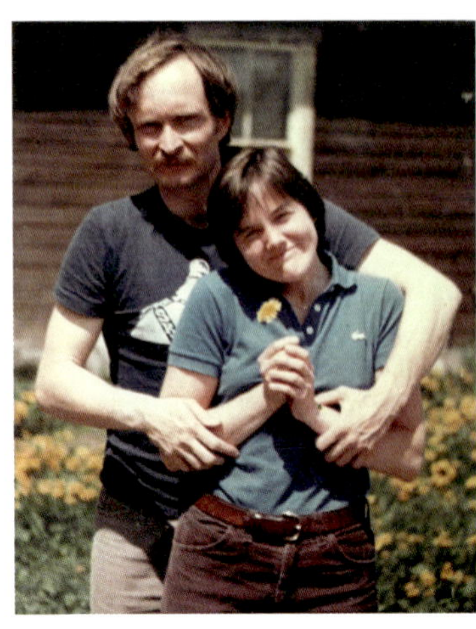

Oh, How I Miss …

Oh, how I miss those arms, those eyes,
that heart.
Wonderfully lanky arms,
so often draped over my shoulder
or linked in mine
as we walked and talked
in harmony and peace.
Beautiful blue eyes,
filled with such tenderness and acceptance,
seeing me as I had never been seen before.
I saw you seeing me and knew that
you saw me seeing you.
Deeply caring heart
so in love with me
and the glories and challenges
of marriage and parenthood shared.
The heart that knew the moment we met
that you and I would be us.
And a wonderful us we were,
still are.
Even in moments of stress or misunderstanding
the promise of
reconciliation and restoration,
no grudges to be held,
remained true.
In my healing I've learned to embrace it all—
triumphs and sorrows,

connection and loneliness,
love and longing.
And, oh how I miss those arms, those eyes,
that heart.

May 15, 2018

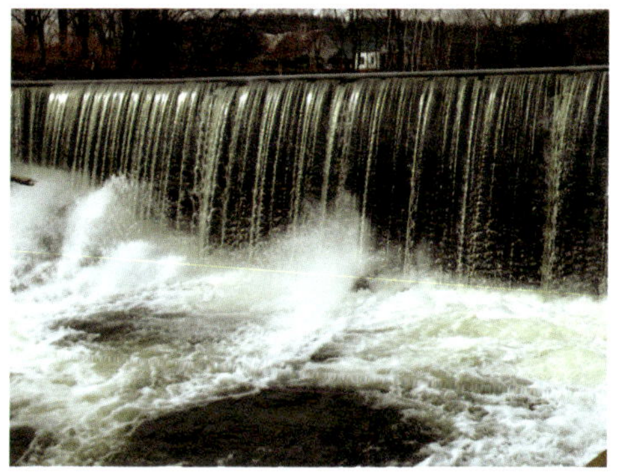

Water Over a Dam

Having gone *there*,
with time spent in varied and intricate
nooks and crannies,
there's the discovery of an amazing energy
that is both novel and familiar.
It has a wildness and yet it's tame,
a fierceness partnered with empathy.
It contains an astonishing gusto
paired with sensations of serenity
that swirl throughout the stream.
Internal exploration
provides for opportunities
to let go, let flow
and produces this
wonderfully eclectic energy.
Healing is a process,
not a singular event.
At times there is a jettison
that is liberating,
feels so very good.
At other times there is confusion,
when what was once regarded as right

transmutes to wrong,
and vice versa.
Like water over a dam
trappings and notions plunge away,
debris carried to places unknown,
while residual vapors hover
to be reintegrated
or let go when the time is right.
Discombobulating,
transforming
invigorating,
reorienting,
liberating.
Water over a dam.

May 17, 2018

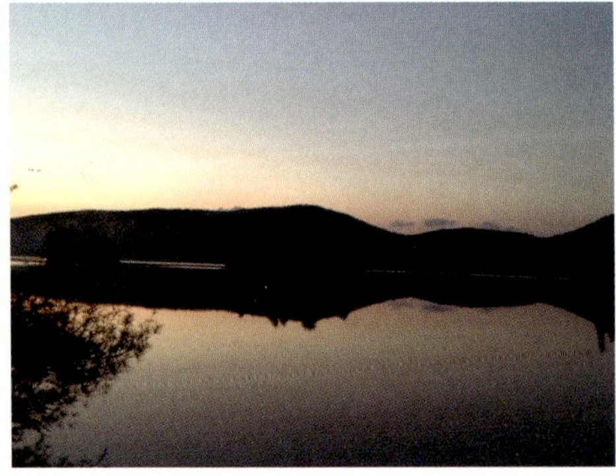

Sweet Little Island

A quiet island sits
surrounded by reflective waters,
evening sky slowly slipping
into darkness.
I, on the edge of the road,
feel drawn to the scene
and so pause to take it in.
Days later I remember,
and realize why I stopped.
More and more I have the
sense of being on my own island
in both the clarity

and uncertainty of life.
This is actually growth,
as I've worked to
adjust to losing the one with whom
I felt safe navigating
varied currents and inevitable obstacles.
My island is part of a whole
and I am included in the
tender loving support of the Divine.
I know that.
There are moments when I
have to draw in to
protect my shoreline
and interior landscape
as I continue to internalize that
I don't have to be a repository
for the hurts and sorrows of others.
This is not easy for one with a caring heart,
inquisitive mind,
sensitive soul.
It is, however, vital to healing.
I'm going to need more time
to fully unlearn a habit that
was so deeply in place.
If I need to pull up,
take shelter on the sweet little island
that is me—
so be it.
Though loneliness does visit,
it's a wonderful place to be,
safe in the knowledge
that I am loved.

May 20, 2018

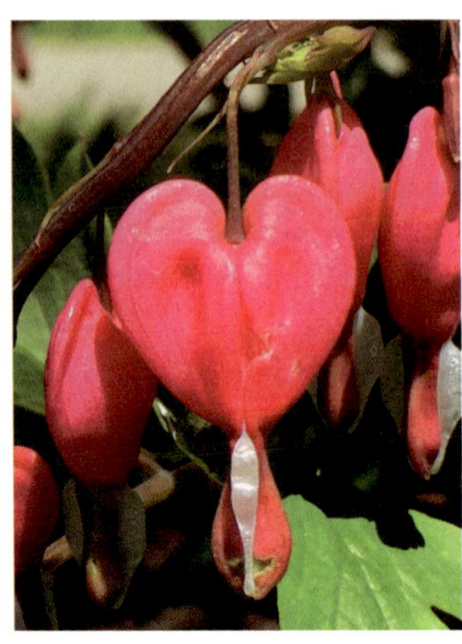

Nothing to Do

Sometimes there's nothing one can do.
I'm going to have to let that notion
sink all the way in.
For so long I took on far more than I should.
It wasn't necessarily wrong at the time and
I learned a great deal in the trying.
There are things I know about me,
about life and healing,
that I may not have internalized
any other way.
These recognitions are part of
a pivotal juncture in my life.
They came to me as I settled onto my island
and some winds began to bellow,
congesting the scene,
making my airways tighten.
They weren't deeply threatening,
just stirred things up and pestered.
I tuned in for a bit and then realized I could
take shelter with my boundaries strong,
allow for internal reorganization,
turn both away and to.
As I quieted I thought back
to the last night, 16 years ago,
when Barry and I were still us in the flesh.
We walked arm in arm around our neighborhood,
out for an evening stroll in the sweet spring air,

teenage children at home.
The next morning three of us raced off to school
and he, on vacation, met some friends
for a game of tennis.
And then it happened.
He died.
With this habit of feeling
that there must be something I can do,
could have done,
I deeply internalized fault.
Did he try to tell me something on our walk?
How could I not have known?
What did I miss?
But he didn't,
I couldn't,
and I didn't miss a thing.
There was nothing to do,
but be in the moments as we were,
cherish each other as we did,
and be in love.
Another radiant change—
acknowledging that
I didn't make a mistake
because there really was
nothing to do.
Sometimes there just isn't.

May 29, 2018

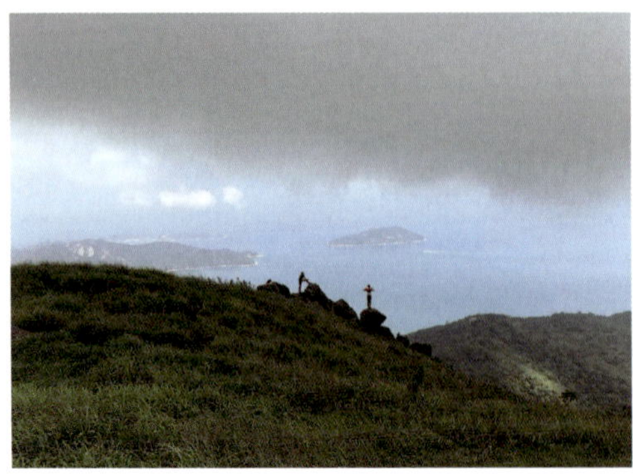

Unique and Yet the Same

Perched upon rocks left askew by
earthly forces of bygone days—
solitary and together, both.
Awestruck, they widen their gazes,
enabling splendor and accomplishment
to saturate.
Breathing in, they watch the ocean
loosen its grip as
the once pervasive fog rises,
revealing treasured islands below.
They pause in wonder,
allowing gratitude to
permeate their beings
before they put feet to ground
and move on.
They follow the meandering trail
to the village far below,
ready for a time of
rest and rejuvenation
as new adventures await.
Sinewy singing muscles,
tranquil trusting minds,
beautiful beating hearts.
Unique and yet the same.

June 5, 2018

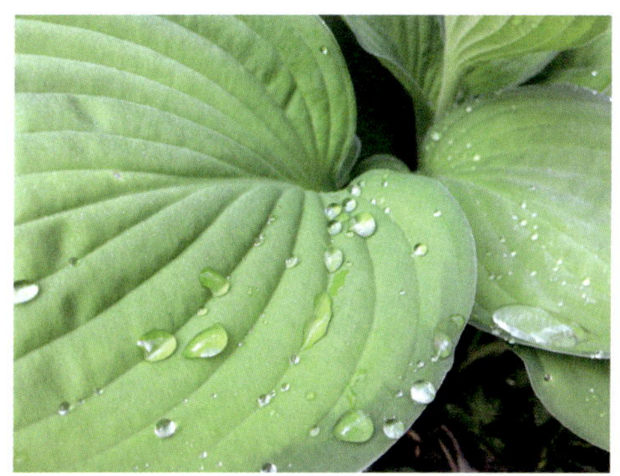

Mourning Dew

Expanding essence,
settling spirit,
vibrating vitality—
a trilogy of wellness.
Even with these truths aboard,
sadness sometimes
seeps to the surface,
quietly gathers
for acknowledgment.
For it is also true,
real, and right.
Like morning dew on
leaves and grasses,
stale sorrows bead and adhere
until a being notices,
allows them to vaporize
or entwine with
restoration and revival.
Mourning dew,
warmed by
mourning light.
A gentle,
beneficial aspect
of the continued
honoring of the
veracity of grief.

June 8, 2018

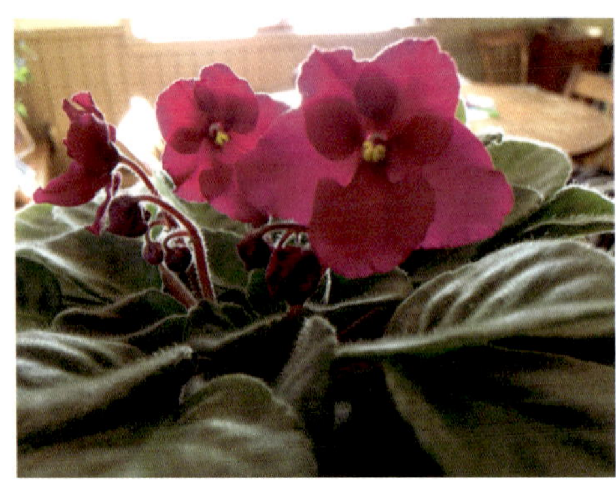

No Longer a Threat

A hole in the screen,
a break in the skin,
a door left open.
A worry that something will
infiltrate, infect, fester.
A constant sense of jeopardy
rooted in origins
both understood and not.
This powerful effect of the wound
is losing its potency
as boundaries are determined
and continue to fortify
in such a way as to allow
benevolent permeability.
All the while, the true taproot
grows stronger
with life-giving liquids circulating
more and more freely.
Mind settling,
heart nurturing,
soul fostering—
dynamic and sure
they surge and swirl,
providing a fullness
that is at the same time
fresh and familiar.
Truth spirals,
grace expands,
love swells,

and there simply is
no longer a threat.

June 19, 2018

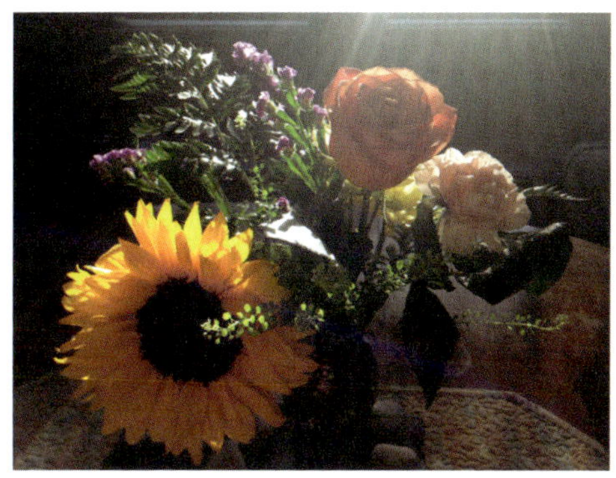

Full Light

Sunbeams stretch and reach
all beings below,
warm and enlighten
those who choose to notice
and let it all in,
let it all out.
Darker days, mere memories
of the cold winter season,
have beauty and substance
all their own.
Day by day the light has grown
to reach the vibrancy
of the Solstice.
Fullness without,
fullness within.
Full Light.

June 21, 2018

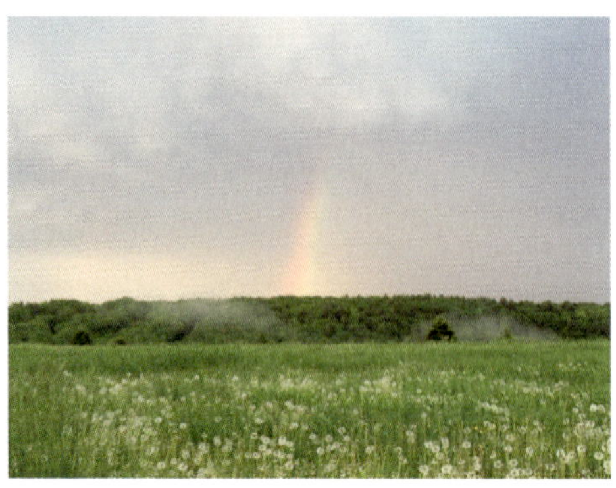

Lonely, Yet Not

I am supposed to feel loneliness right now.
I know this because within this feeling
I am more profoundly discovering me,
my veritable, essential self.
The one who has been there all along,
but had to struggle to exist within
confusing, imposed falseness.
She is lovely and strong,
caring and humble,
creative and intelligent,
graceful and giving.
I love her
and know she is
not really alone.
Tears are flowing from
deep in my soul.
I don't necessarily have words
to accompany them,
but they do need to flow.
So I let them
and, in tandem,
feel the elation
of settling into the exquisite
recesses of my being.
I am solo right now
with summer here and
no students who need me,
offspring grown
with lives of their own,
soulmate's physical presence gone.

It's okay,
I need this.
I've worked hard
to land here
in this very spot.
It's a bit stormy
but I've got it.
I'm lonely,
yet not.

June 24, 2018

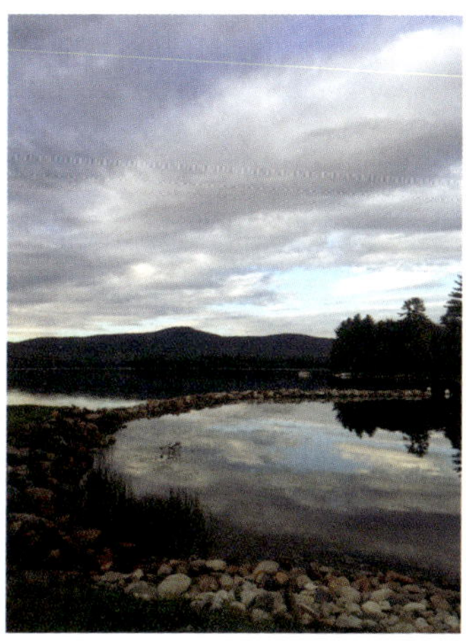

Lighten Up

Eyes, heart,
mind, cells
open wider and wider.
Flexible, changing
frontier becomes
more and more
true and trustworthy.
Sinking, settling
into a precious body,
beautiful just as it is
in the here and now.
Antiquated perceptions
that one must strive to receive love,
must somehow earn the right to heal,

release, steadily melt away.
Moments of "OH!", blips of freedom,
expand and saturate.
Sensations of revival
that feel right and good,
but will take time
to more fully incorporate.
Intrepid, courageous exploration
has paved the way
to understand that the need to 'earn'
came from a deep and barricaded place.
But the freedom, the lightening
comes from an even deeper,
more expansive
place of knowing—
where the light shines through,
always has.
It most definitely is time to
allow the canards to crumble,
honor the hues of healing,
and lovingly
lighten up.

June 26, 2018

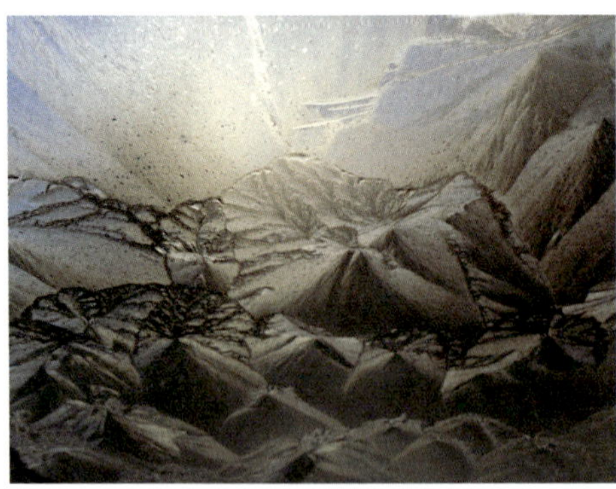

Darkening Before the Light

The whole story
needs to be told.
Before the lightening,
perhaps simultaneous to it being born,

there was/is a sort of darkening.
Tears seep and surge,
seeming to surface
from every part of the body.
Reminiscent of a full-on baby cry
when the only remedy is to be
cuddled, comforted,
with tears accepted, not judged.
Experienced as an adult,
this is accompanied
by multi-faceted grief.
Safe and right to feel,
the eventual effects
are the soothing of a tender heart,
the settling of a puzzled mind,
the mending of a wounded spirit.
A darkening before the light
that has the power to
heal the deep, dark places
that simply must be honored.
It's the truth, the full narrative,
that leads to
a shift from threat to trust,
providing the opportunity
to genuinely lighten up.

June 27, 2018

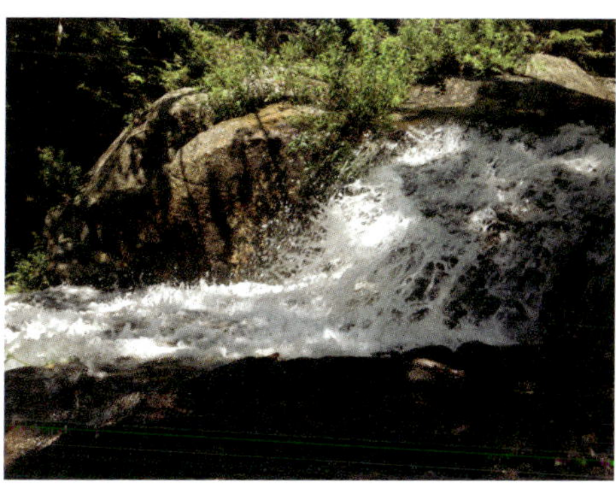

Waves of Fear

I don't really identify with being a fearful person,
and yet I'm feeling waves of fear.

There's a craving within
to realize that I'm safe.
I'm so very ready for these
waves to fully wash away.
I'm sitting here in my sweet little home,
cradled in memories
of sharing love and life with my soulmate,
holding and raising our sweet babies,
finding my way to becoming a teacher.
I can recognize that the body-wracking cries of yesterday
have mostly subsided,
but still feel unheralded emotions stirring
as muscles softly twitch, milder tears trickle,
breath seems shallow.
Like the rain cascading outside these windows,
the gentle breeze that blows,
I guess it just needs to happen.
I don't have to run and hide,
or feel threatened.
I still feel the wish to be held or
at least to hear someone say the words,
"You're okay, Sarah.
It's right to let the those waves of fear
roll out and away.
It's true, you're safe."
I'm hopeful this desire
will fade away over time,
or that I will be able to
comfort that tender spot within
for my self.
I don't think I care anymore
to know exactly
where they originate,
I'm just trying to believe
that waves of fear
simply do not have a place
in my life anymore.

June 28, 2018

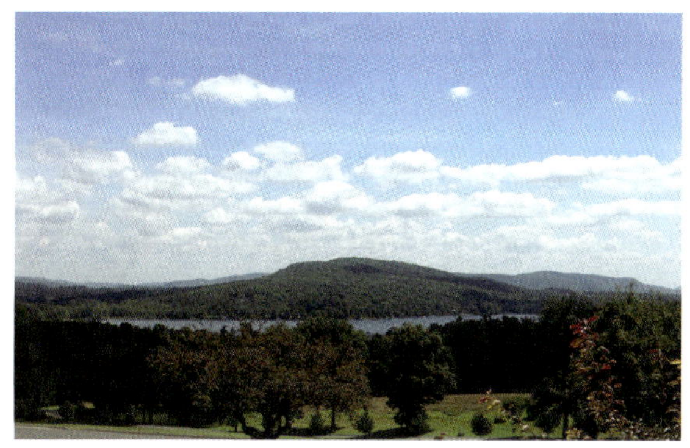

Right Here

Back again—
in the same place, yet not.
Previous insecurities release,
enabling the dropping in
to widen, become more full.
My tapestry of
images and words,
reflecting the radiance of
so many changes,
continues.
Hopes,
once felt to be distant,
gently and continually unfold,
reach fruition.
Impediments still occur,
though they are malleable,
less menacing,
easier to transform to truth.
As I sit and settle,
enfold my vitality,
more and more I appreciate
my singular self.
Having felt unheard,
unseen, unsure
in my past,
I hold tangible evidence
and begin to rest easy.
All that has come
from going in
is real, valid, and right.

I hear, I see,
and I am becoming
more sure.
Those who feel inclined will
listen, notice, acknowledge,
and I shall do the same.
I am right here,
gratefully and gracefully
being me.

July 4, 2018

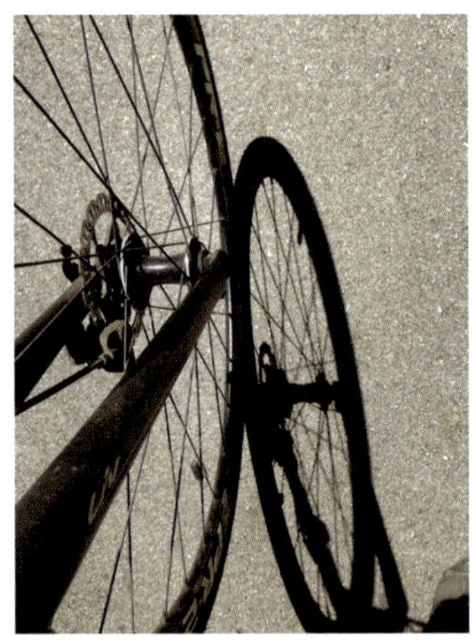

Time to Recharge

Having discharged both things I can define
and things I cannot,
I feel a distinctly different energy.
Some unwanted thought patterns still nibble,
but I find what I need in order
to allay these minor wonderings.
It may simply be speaking them aloud
to someone I trust.
Or it might be enough to take a pause,
breathe, alter the flow.
Other times I simply must write,
let metaphoric experiences
come alive on paper before my eyes.
The letting go is both from me

and to me.
As this shift in energy suffuses,
I believe the places that have emptied
will fill with what I need
and a sense of safety will
mingle and merge
as I recharge.
I think I must be patient,
allow this to happen in its own time.
As it does I sometimes feel happiness spread.
Like a moment at a concert,
with music of days gone by emanating throughout,
noticing that my face feels strange
and realizing it is because I
had been smiling for quite some time.
Or looking down in awe at the shadow
of my bike wheel,
seeing all parts working in tandem,
powered by me.
I know I've shown great
strength and courage along the way.
This is about opening wide to Universal Love,
letting the recharge happen as it will.
No threat, no shame, no reason to hide.
Simply time to recharge.

July 10, 2018

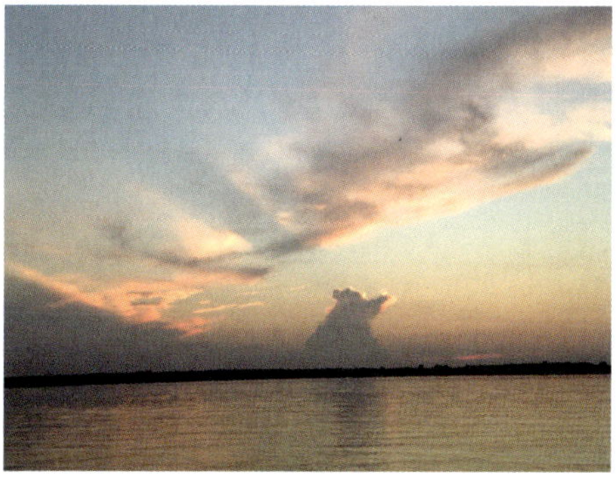

One Degree

I've spent some time twisting my lens
over the years,

have become quite adept at it.
At this point turning it as little as
one degree provides
a gentle sense of clarity and relief
that is both rightful and welcome.
Simple, quiet moments
when what was just barely out of focus
becomes crystal clear,
melds into healing.
This is like being bathed
in a subtle, calm lightness
that both buoys and cleanses.
Or it can be a spreading sense
of fortitude that has long been there,
but feels more apparent and credible.
I often don't even know that I'm adjusting,
but recognize the blips of awareness.
Like when the sun is at a perfect angle
so muted shadows stretch into
a summer twilight sky
as soft clouds billow
and you happen to gaze upwards
at just the right time.
Sweet sensations of
wonder and awe ascend,
the moment both fleeting
and timeless.
Safety and serenity reside
within and without
and all is well.

July 23, 2018

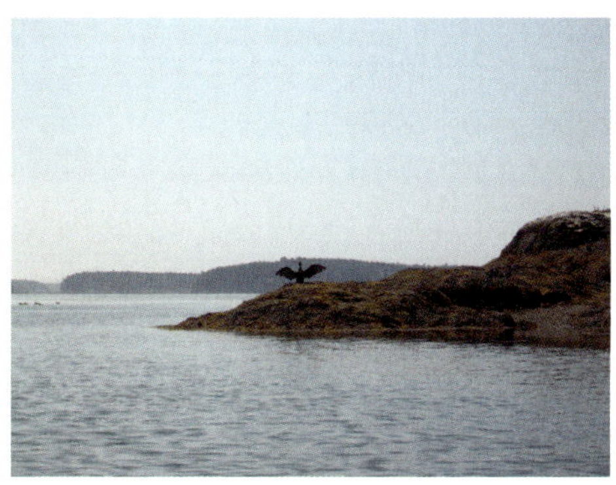

Liberty

Suspended in salty goodness,
she lays back and relaxes.
Gazing upward she marvels
at the blueness of the sky,
glowing warmth of the sun,
soft clouds flowing gently by.
She breathes in the fresh, warm air,
allowing her lungs to fill as they will.
All is in motion and yet
there is nothing that needs doing,
not right at that moment anyway.
Her mind wanders and she remembers
swimming as a child
when her nickname was 'Fish'.
She smiles as she thinks back to
that lovely little girl,
so comfortable under the water
as she frolicked in the waves.
A quiet frown comes as she feels
residual fear stir,
but then there's a release
as she realizes they are free from all that.
Just as the tides disperse detritus,
so can all that go.
And just as the richness of the
expansive ocean fills back in,
so can she allow the bounty to come.
Another deep breath
as she feels vitality, peace, and love.
The tides flow, come and go,

in freedom.
More and more she feels safe to enfold
the liberty
of her own tides
within.

July 24, 2018

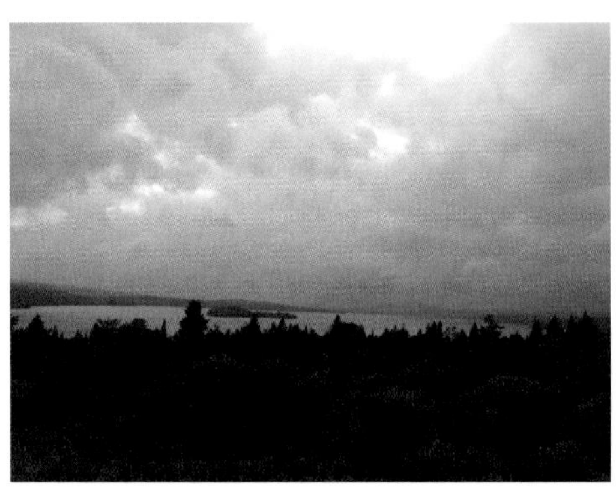

Sweet, Soft Memories

Up and over Dallas Hill,
along the ridge,
is the little red house we called home
when our first baby was born.
Down the other side,
on the shore of Saddleback Lake,
is where our love first emerged.
I visited this special part
of our world,
and as I explored,
the pain of loss was very gentle.
Instead I was filled
with sweet, soft memories
of tennis matches, moonlight hikes,
bike rides to the movies,
horseback adventures—
me riding Buck, you astride Fire,
as we opened our hearts
to each other.
Before I headed down the road
to return to the home we shared

as our children grew,
I gazed out over the lake.
And again delightful memories
swirled all through.
Paddling, sailing, swimming,
skiing on the frozen surface.
I will always miss your physical presence,
but these memories are
such a tender balm to my being
as I harbor them
in my healing heart.
I'm so grateful for
sweet, soft memories
of you and me
together.

July 29, 2018

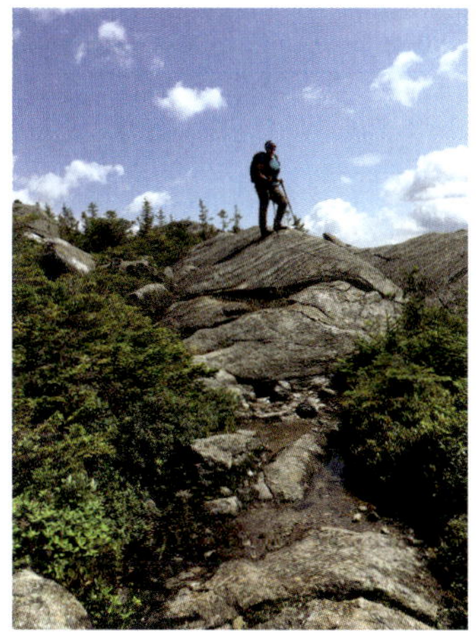

Truth

Hear me, little one.
Trust me when I say you are safe,
we are safe.
We've worked hard
to uncover and explore,
wonder and weep,
receive and recover.
We, together, are me

and it's time to fully align to the truth.
The continual sense of goodness
that has kept me company,
even in the hardest of times,
is real.
The core of strength
that has fortified my being
all along the way
is sure.
The ability to write,
illuminating healing and hope,
is beautiful and right to share.
The curative experiences
of body, mind, and spirit
can and should
be welcomed and absorbed.
On solid ground,
beneath a benign sky,
serenaded by flowing waters
I stand full, robust, and ready.
I can take deep restorative breaths,
open wide to the beauty
both before me and within me.
Though there may be occasional stirs
as I assimilate and adjust,
the truth is
I am safe
to freely, fully,
firmly
be me.

August 6, 2018

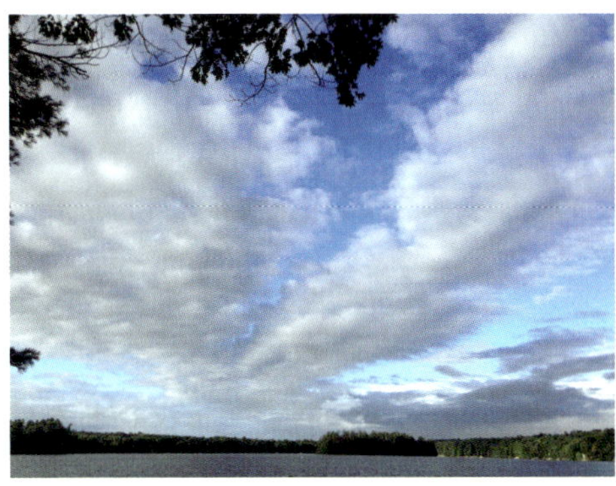

There Again

We went there again.
To the old gray camp that is so close,
yet so far, from home.
I know you were unsure about going.
I don't blame you.
But you trusted,
allowed in the safety of now.
I felt your tenseness as we entered the kitchen
through the creaky screen door.
But you started to relax
as we reached the living room,
sensing the difference
in the atmosphere of the place.
You checked every nook and cranny
with your eyes and your heart,
especially the open porch
with lake breezes wafting around and through.
You so badly wanted the changes
to be real, to be true.
As you turned and walked toward the pantry
you stopped in your tracks,
taking it in anew.
It was altered
in both appearance and energy,
all traces of alcohol gone,
along with associated tension and angst.
Really, truly no longer there.
I felt your tender essence
infuse with hope, faith, delight—
your face aglow, your eyes a-twinkle,

your body at ease.
Yes, we went there again.
To that place of sadness,
misunderstanding,
and generational suffering.
It took some doing,
but we were solid and sure,
happy in our health,
able to fully accept the veracity of what is,
allow the ferocity of musty memories to wane.
Those dark days are done,
no longer need to produce pain.
Later, sitting by the lake,
watching the clouds drift above
and the loons swim by,
residual wariness and worry slid away,
replaced with love
and gratitude for having gone
there again.

August 8, 2018

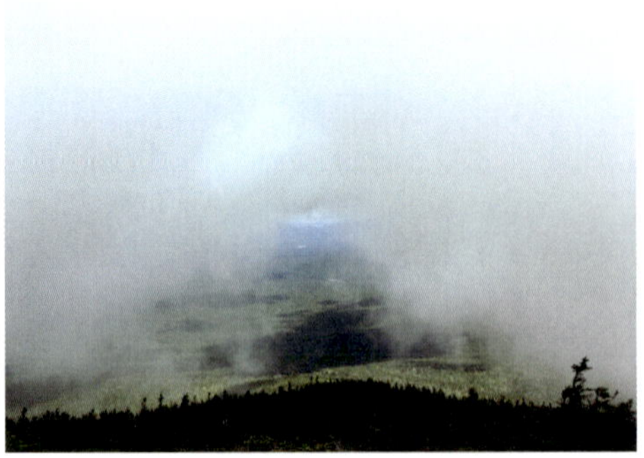

Cloud Bath

To the top of a favorite mountain
at the invitation of new friends.
Yet again,
I put one foot in front of the other
and make my way.
More sure-footed this time,
with far less tension in my body,

very little ache in my heart.
To the summit we stretch,
and beyond.
On a rocky prominence we perch,
in awe of the lovely view.
In the distance
other mountains visited,
lakes enjoyed,
roads biked.
This busy body content
to simply sit, breathe, be.
Varied clouds
flow with summery breezes,
natural cinema playing
before our eyes.
Some vapors settle
in the basin behind,
begin to sweep up the back slope.
Hugging the col,
they roll over the ridge,
descend the front slope
before they lift,
rise up as if in jubilation
at their freedom.
We humans immerse
in a cloud bath
with a smooth, gentle power.
Honored to be right there
in those moments,
I welcome the chance
for quiet cleansing and
soothing rejuvenation.

August 15, 2018

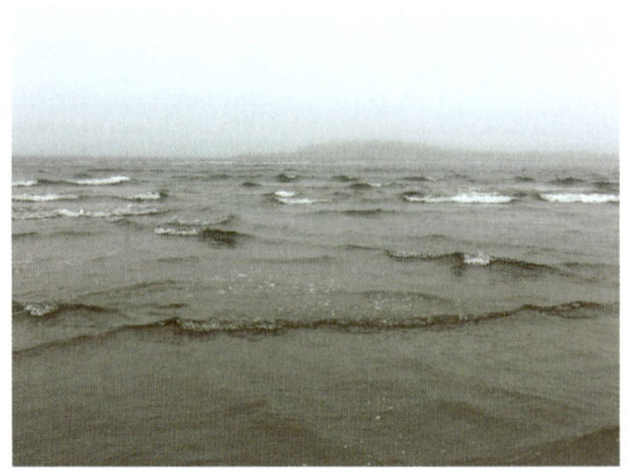

Two Briny Beings

Standing strong
in soft sand,
my tender feet
sink just a bit.
Ocean waves come from
multiple directions,
wash around my legs.
I am mesmerized by the moment,
though I don't quite know why.
I just knew I needed to be
right there, right then.
I can still feel the sensations of
sand caressing my feet,
water enveloping my skin.
Two briny beings
in a tidal dance
of wholeness.
I didn't have to understand fully
the reasons for my desire to
be in that spot,
just knew to follow the guidance
from whence it came.
No tension, no worry,
no remorse.
That sublime sensation
of letting go,
letting flow
in action once again
around me,

for me,
within me.

August 15, 2018

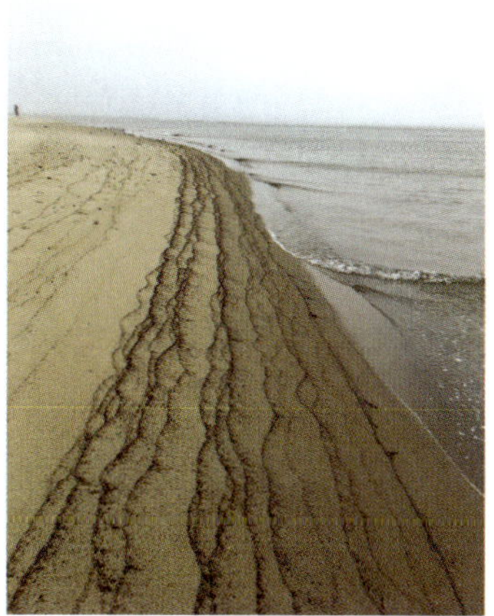

Ancestral Angst

Some of the energy from ancestral angst
somehow settled within.
Part of my lineage
with a distinct rigidity
that I've lugged
for a long while.
As I heal, the strands often loosen,
discharging tension.
It's as if there's a conduit
to sorrows of the past
to which I am linked,
but with current that is lessening.
Because these bonds are so old
there can be a bit of a skirmish
as they let go,
I let go.
Sometimes I think I should apologize,
which in moments of release
makes no sense at all.
Perhaps I am sorry because I care,
but now know that the issues

of my forebears were theirs,
not mine.
Maybe I'm just sorry because
distress was such a large
piece of the puzzle
as I remember it,
took it in.
I'm not sorry that I recognized
my need for liberation.
As more and more unloads,
washes away,
I access greater appreciation for
the goodness of the grains
that also form my foundation,
and theirs.
I'm sure they didn't mean to
cause family fracture.
I'll never fully understand
all that was broken,
but I do know that
none of it was my fault.
Though I still meander back,
I am acutely aware that
whatever happened is over.
I can flow forward with relief
at being
less and less connected
to ancestral angst.

August 18, 2018

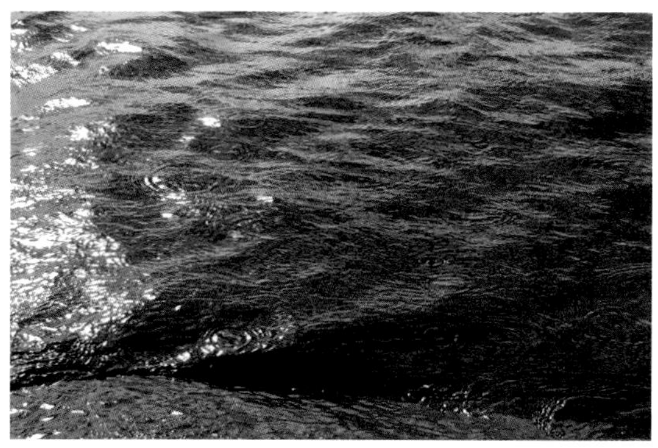

Sun Shimmers and Rain Plops

Blue-gray sky speckled with fair weather clouds.
Just enough wind to make evergreens waltz,
waves lap against my granite perch,
sunlight glitter upon their varied faces.
I settle in to read for a bit,
about indigenous wisdom and
the illusion of separation.
In need of some time
to ponder the message
I set my book aside and,
from seemingly nowhere,
a gentle, spotty rain begins to fall.
For just a few moments
sun shimmers and rain plops
dance on the water's surface,
together as one.
Circles within circles,
bobbing, expanding, flowing
on the twinkling, reflective sheen.
Grateful and content,
I smile at nature's
timely illustration.

August 26, 2018

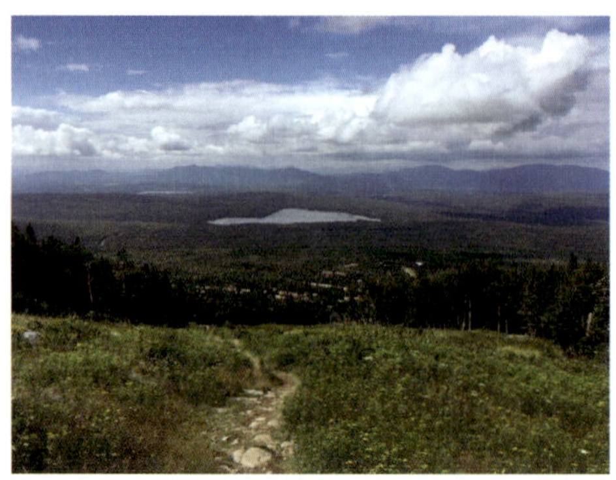

The Way Ahead

Our stories intersect.
We criss-cross each other
as we meet, greet, be.
Some stories entwine us
more than others,
like the story of true, deep, shared love.
The soulmate kind.
A sturdy anchor that can
keep a vessel secure
despite varied pulls.
When, for whatever reason,
the physical container of that love leaves,
there's a scary sensation
of being adrift
and vulnerable.
It's easy to hold on to
that which actually constricts,
promotes tension within.
Part of healing from the angst
and emptiness
of being on that drifty ship
involves learning how and when
to let go.
There can be a sense of others
having power over you,
when in truth they don't.
You might feel beholden,
responsible,
or simply wrong
at times when you are

stretching into your newness.
What a profound, liberating moment when
you realize
that you can let go,
even of that.
When you do,
the way ahead becomes
even more hopeful, open,
and true.

August 28, 2018

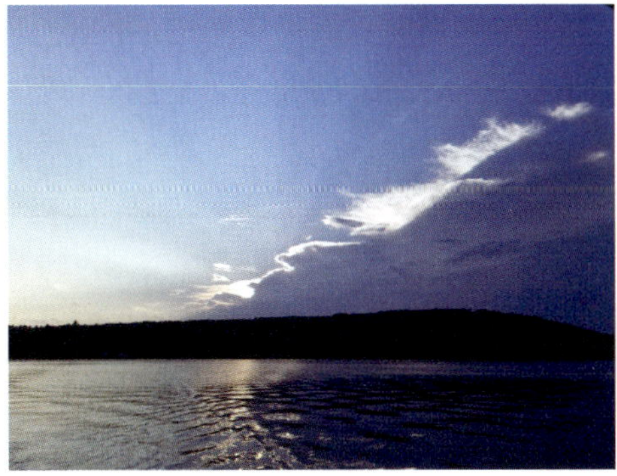

Allow

Some clouds are stormy,
some benign,
some hard to read.
And yet the sun has the potential
to illuminate the edges
of them all,
given the right conditions.
Just as our nearest star
facilitates the splendor
of silver linings,
so can we humans permit our
inner brilliance to shine
from behind whatever
barricades may be in place.
We all want to,
though the desire may be
somewhat sequestered.

No matter what fronts
have blown through,
our own exquisite uniqueness
is there nestled within,
ours to share when
we feel secure and right.
And that we should—
both feel safe
and allow.
The sun doesn't hesitate.
Why should we?

September 11, 2018

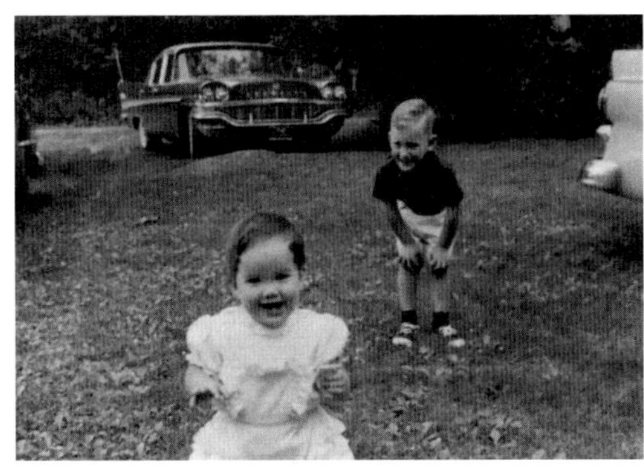

Marvel With Me

Dear Geof,
I wish I could talk with you
about so many things
that have been on my mind lately.
You are the only one
who shared tender,
sometimes tremulous,
childhood years with me.
It's been so long
since we sat in the garden
as young adults
marveling at our spouses,
our little ones.
That was the last day,
me just turned 30

and you 33.
Hmm, I just realized
that we didn't actually
talk much right then.
But in those moments
our energies merged
and we were content.
You used to insist that
the things that were broken
were not mine to fix.
I don't know how you knew that
at such a young age,
but you were right.
It feels so very good to
more and more let go
of that assumed responsibility.
As I do
my whole being loosens
and I can recall
joyful memories like
having a big brother
marvel with me.

Love, Sarah
September 16, 2018

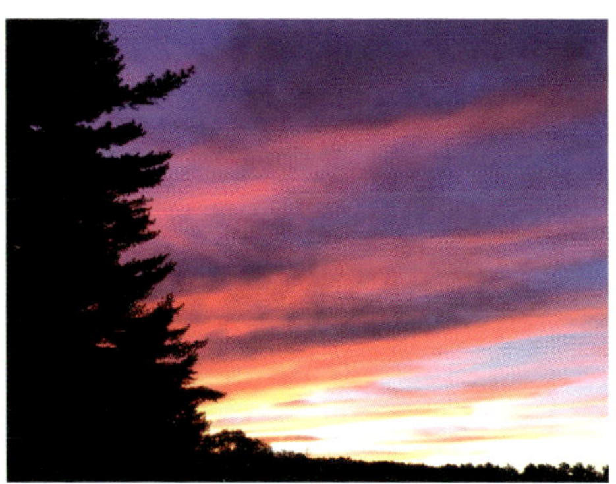

Boundless Expanse

It takes some work to uncover your fathoms,
especially if they've been ensconced for long.
There may be layers that are confusing

or weigh a great deal.
You may not always recognize the fabric
of the coverings
as opportunities to lift them appear.
But lift them you should.
Carefully, tenderly raise them
when you are ready.
The setting aside is not always predictable.
You might need to spread the material out
so you can take a closer look.
Or maybe you'll need to gently fold it
as you reminisce,
continue to assimilate.
Some layers should be shared
with a trusted confidante
so you can further process their effects.
And then there are those pieces
you'll need to fling aside,
perhaps even rip them to shreds,
let them scatter
in the winds of change.
But the insights that come from your efforts
are most definitely miraculous.
Along the way you will gradually
see, hear, feel things more purely
and enjoy being uniquely you.
The spiky intricacies
of whatever your dark times include
will either disperse or
peacefully coexist with the glory
of the boundless expanse that contains
wonder, truth, communion
and Love.

September 25, 2018

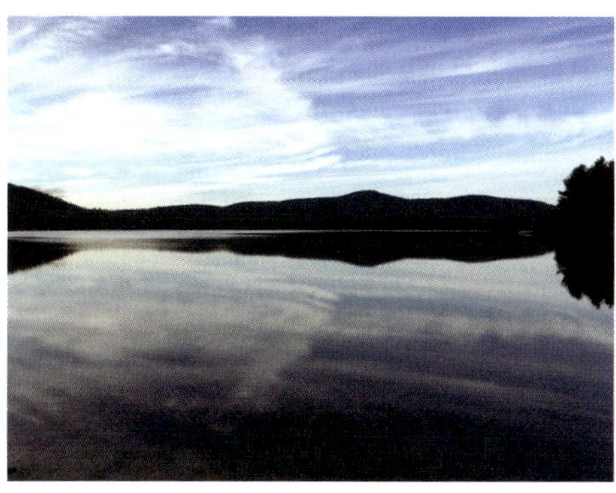

Coming Undone

It's coming undone
and I'm so glad.
The tether that kept me bound
to a multi layered,
completely false sense of responsibility
is frayed and tattered,
only has a few tired strands left.
I'm somewhat in awe
at how well I've navigated
with that crusty anchor
dragging, twisting, snagging.
What a heavy load,
fastened before I knew any better.
At times it is crystal clear
when someone wrongly tries to process
their own stuff through me.
In some ways I seem to be
a bit of a magnet for that.
But, I no longer accept that position
and I'm getting better
at kindly and gently
fending it off.
It's the subtle times,
when others almost seem devious
in their attempts to pass the buck,
that still drag me down.
I don't always catch it
as deep sediments get stirred and
that which reflects back
seems murky and muddled,

doesn't match what I know to be true.
Eventually, though, I figure it out,
acknowledge another opportunity to mend.
These last strands,
the inner weave of the tether,
may take more time to let go.
Or, not.
Either way is fine.
I'm just profoundly grateful that it's
coming undone.

October 9, 2018

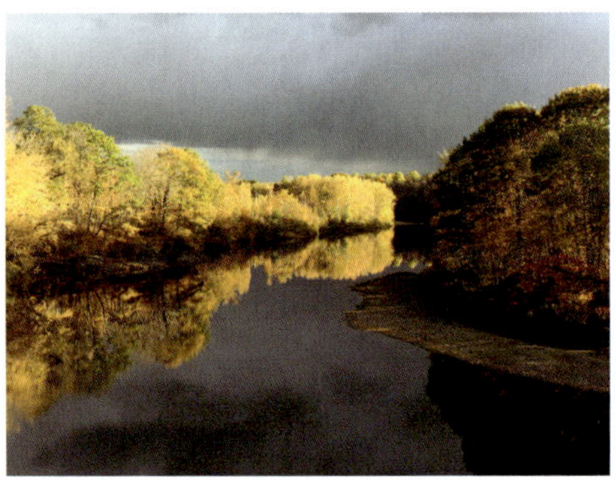

Autumn Afternoon

(abecedarius)

Autumn afternoon pedaling on my trusty
bike. Blustery winds blow some rain in, but I don't
care. I'm in the rhythm of riding as varied thoughts
dance through my mind.
Eventually you enter and, as always, I'm grateful that you
find your way in. It has become a
gentle sense of joining as I work to
harness the shifting energies of healing, the
intricate undertones and sometimes bewildering
juxtaposition of openness and boundaries. The
kinesthetic nature of pedaling
leads to connections of heart and
mind. As my gears hum I
notice my health and feel grateful, not
only for when we were us in the flesh, but also for sensations of your

presence now. I pause on the bridge near our home, smile with knowing that my
quirky
rogue dead guy continues to show up, sometimes murky and other times clear,
sensations of love shared always present. I've had some
trying times lately, have had to strive to
understand. It's been a bit painful, really, but with
visceral relief distinctly present. I have more
work to do, but it's actually
e**x**hilarating to be here right now, in me. I continue to honor
your love as I let my
zeal out into the light of day and decide what reflections I want to let in.

October 13, 2018

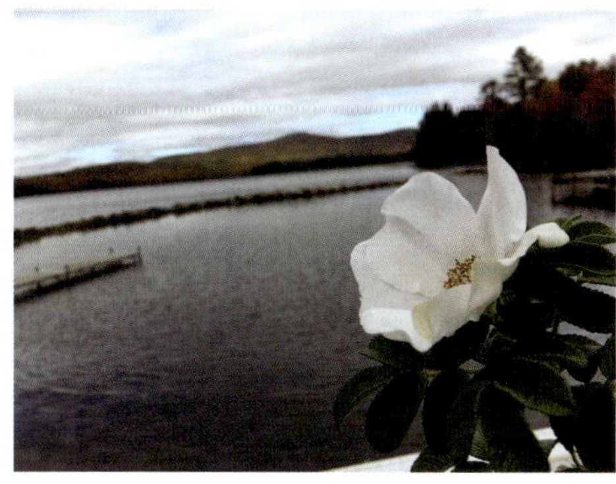

Blossoming

Tiny one lays on her back,
wide open to the newness
of the world around her.
All she really needs is sustenance,
tenderness, the security
of a sense of place.
She exudes the joy of living
just by being herself.
But every so often
something is off,
not quite right.
Her beautiful being tenses
as she cries out,
looks toward the one
who might offer solace.

But it's not there
and so she begins to master
the tucking away of suffering.
Now,
so many years later,
she can still feel
the deep, stale discomfort of
the missing
and the hiding.
But she also again recognizes
opportunity to unlearn and relearn,
orient to a source of love
that is boundless,
trustworthy,
and true.
She closes her eyes,
carefully lays open once again
as, bit by bit,
that antiquated source of fear and pain
fades into the distance,
softening as it goes.
Her focus shifts to
the grace and haven of
blossoming.

October 24, 2018

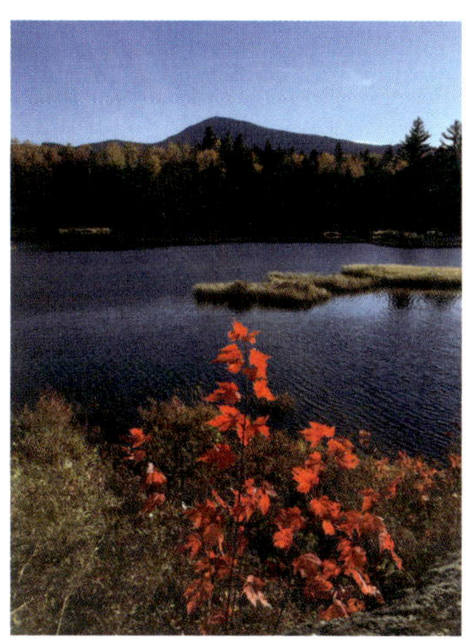

Greater Than, Less Than, Equal To

Numbers—
so concrete,
easy to compare.
One definitely worth either
more than, less than,
or the same as another.
It's clear what their relationship is,
once you know the rules
and how they operate.
And then there's us,
we humans,
with our varied and complex interweavings.
It is so often said that we are all created equal,
yet there are those who seem to believe
they are greater than,
constantly needing that 'fact'
to be seen.
Likely they may actually feel less than
somewhere deep within,
and so the need to prove.
By stepping out into the natural world
it's easy to behold true equity and balance.

Fledgling tree with changing leaves
sways in a cool fall breeze,
waters of a nearby pond
ruffle and reflect,

mountain backdrop stands
full, strong, and steady.
One part of the scene no greater
or less than the other,
each having an equal part in the grandeur.
The human who takes a pause to notice
fills with the clean, clear energy
of that equality.
Once again grateful
for the teachings of nature,
she moves forward
with more clarity on board.

October 27, 2018

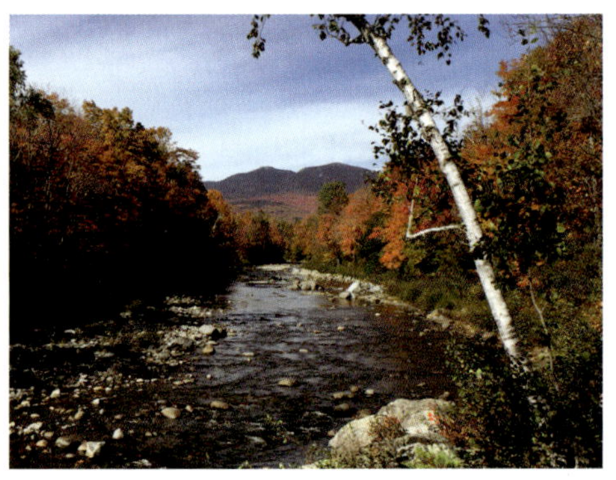

Expanding Faith

Softly, more softly she settles,
trusting that whatever she feels
is rightful
and hers.
One strong, residual strand
of the tether that held her back
weakens all the way,
releases—
the one that made her
feel wrong for needing help.
She finds herself gently reaching,
though she knows not what for,
then realizes it doesn't matter.
In moments of profound healing

whatever happens simply does—
to her, with her, for her.
There's no need to try so hard,
nothing that needs doing
other than allow and accept.
Another turning point,
she feels her cells shimmer,
as the once persistent
sense of jeopardy slides away.
She breathes deep a curative breath,
slowly lets it weave around and through
that which has sparked within.
Her vapors
fan those inner embers once again,
but this time
she doesn't feel constriction
or any need to hold back.
Carefree and peaceful
she breathes again,
and again,
and again.
Pristine energy,
deeper safety, definitive support
partner this liberation.
Heartened by a continually
expanding faith
in unconditional Love,
her inner compass orients
to the fuller and fuller flowing
of the truth of her being.

November 7, 2018

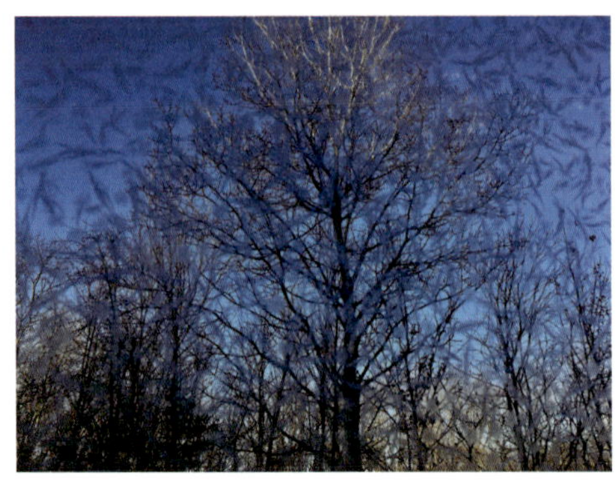

Softly, More Softly

So often we are in a rush.
Do this, solve that,
make it better … now.
But, in truth,
that which is worth exploring
often takes time to fully comprehend.
Instinct helps me allow and encourage this
as the amazing young beings
in my classroom ebb, flow,
gather, and grow—
each in his or her
impeccably unique way.
Why, then, do I feel
I must hurry?
Why am I, the teacher,
often dashing to get from
here to there?
Why do I, the author,
think I must scramble to make sure
my words and images fly
out of the boxes,
off the shelves?
What causes the healing me to
sometimes wonder about failing
if I don't fully enfold newness
right away?
This educator, this author,
this sparkling woman
knows that
illumination is like the

twisting of a kaleidoscope,
pieces cascading, nestling,
settling anew—
beauty at every turn.
So I'm going to make sure to
notice the light
shining wherever it does,
allow understanding
to come as it will,
acknowledge the elegance and grace
that are right before my eyes
each and every day.
I am going to choose to
slow down,
softly, more softly
occupy my own space
in this harried world.

November 18, 2018

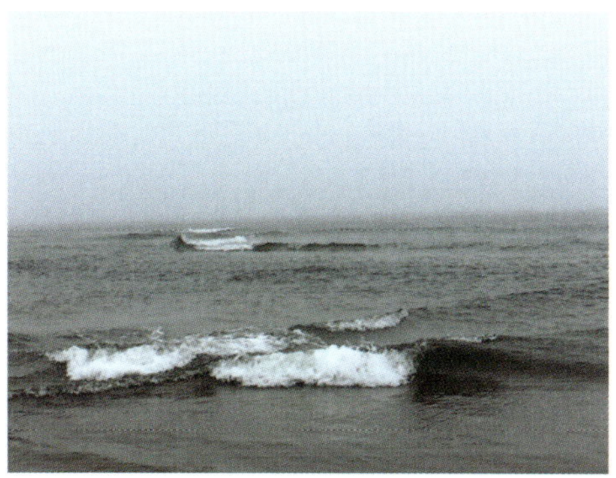

Tranquil, Wide Horizon

Two ships sail on a foggy sea,
their courses diverge.
One heads to brighter, freer days,
the other set to travel
in the same unending denseness.
Its cargo includes
drums of despair,
heaps of heartache,
barrels and barrels of burdens.

With feet firmly planted on
the deck of my own ship,
I raise a steady hand,
wave a misty-eyed good bye.
Those on the deck,
at the helm,
of that galleon of gloom
had brightness mingled with
their shadows,
but distress and tension reigned.
I was on that ship for a time,
my caring heart,
loving nature
groomed to lug a load
that was not mine.
I had to disembark,
climb aboard a ship of my own—
not an easy feat.
Though my shoulders still ache
from the strain of those years,
I carry gratitude
as more and more I discern
transcendent, lively
treasures within.
That dark ship has sailed.
My voyage continues as I look
to the tranquil, wide horizon that beckons.
I hear the gentle waves,
marvel at the starry sky of night,
feel the warmth of
continually emerging light
wafting over the welcoming seascape.
I breathe deep the refreshing air,
fill with acceptance,
wellness, and love.

November 22, 2018
Thanksgiving

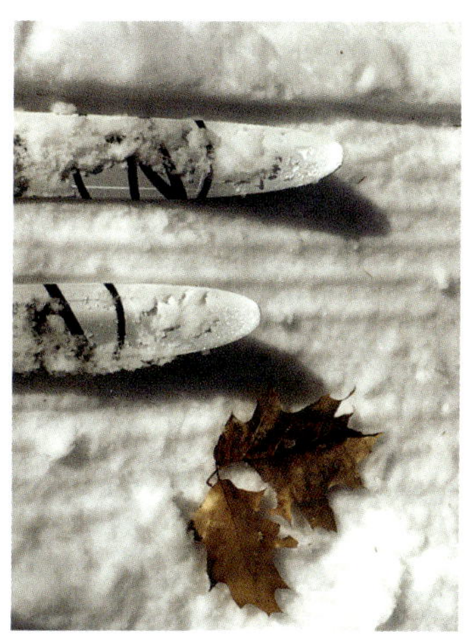

Simply Still

Whether striding ahead with gusto,
taking small exploratory steps,
or pausing to take it all in,
progress comes,
healing happens.
Even meandering
back to what was,
seeing it anew,
supports growth.
Withered leaves fall,
swirling winds blow,
water continues its cycle
even when frozen
on the ground.
Changes,
some obvious
in their radiance,
others sweetly subtle,
continuously occur.
Forward
is often considered
to be moving
straight ahead,
but, in reality,
is in varied directions
and includes interludes.

Expansion can and will happen
when you free yourself to be
simply still.

November 27, 2018

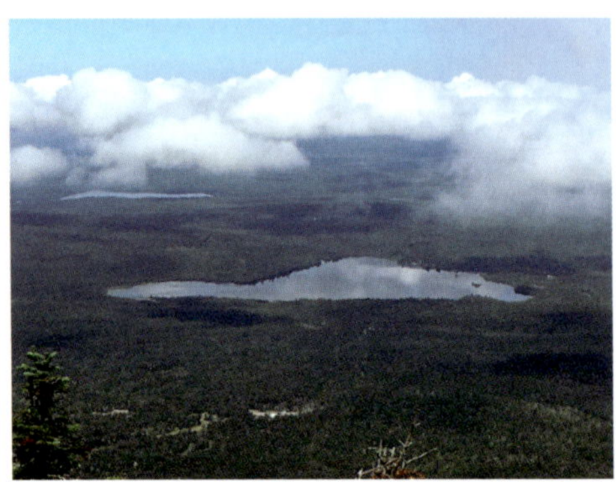

Serene Lake Within

Along the shores of a placid lake,
next to a lovely little cabin,
the world as she knew it erupted
in both scary sights
and vicious sounds.
Her tender, 7-year-old essence
was deeply impacted in those moments.
She remembers the event,
how she and her brother retreated
as far away as they could.
She doesn't remember
any words between them,
just the shared energy of
fear, shock, and wonder—
not the good kind.
She remembers being glad he was there,
now wishes he were still here
so they could recover together.
She doesn't remember
how the quarrel began,
or any talking to process it after.
She does remember
skirmishes that led up to it,

and feeling defeated
in her multiple attempts
at making things right
in the years that followed.
Her adult mind drifts
to another tranquil lake where
her life was again altered,
this time by Love.
In the here and now,
she is profoundly grateful for
the tenderness of that Love,
her ongoing insights from
rising above the fray,
and her growing sense of unity
with the Divine.
She feels an inner stillness,
her very own serene lake within,
free from the confusing undercurrents
of that long ago battle
and its turbulent aftermath.

December 1, 2018

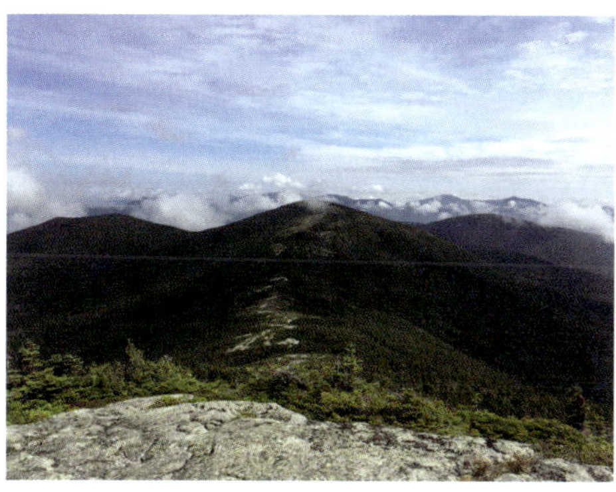

Above the Fray

Ah … sweet freedom.
Riding thermals on strengthening wings
with time and space to
observe, glean, release.
Circling for the sheer joy
of making a turn,

feeling forces at play,
allowing winds of change
to work their magic.
Pristine images of nature-speak
provide opportunity for
twisting the lens as needed.
Vibrant body, calm mind, settled heart
meld together as
residual tension wisps away.
She realizes she may never
know the whole story.
And yet,
she rises—
clearly, freely, uniquely
above the fray,
secure in the knowledge that
whatever the origin,
it was theirs,
not hers.
She knows that life will
contain new challenges
along the way.
But, whatever caused
that particular darkness
is over.
She can
and will
let it
be so.

December 4, 2018

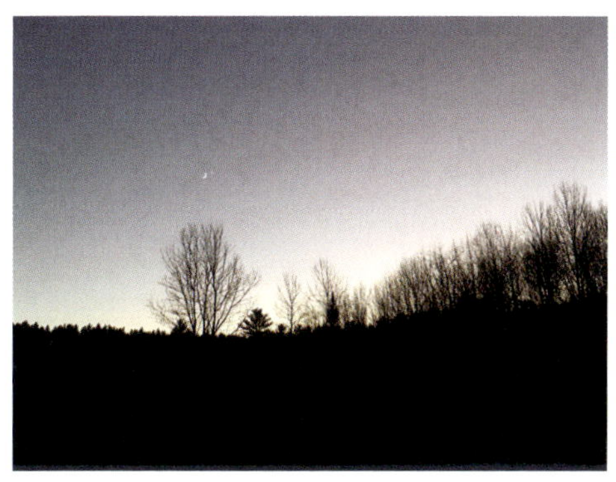

Wintry Twilight

Crisp air, crunchy snow, waning light,
solstice looming.
I rush to fit in a quick ski
after an energizing,
yet tiring day.
Tension slips away as
my skis glide on the grooming.
The familiar fullness
that comes
in the company of trees
and sky
and self locomotion
feels welcome.
I stop for a moment to
breathe it all in,
gazing up
to a crescent moon
drifting above
bare branches
as they tickle
the wintry twilight sky.
Gratefully
I slide
into the evening.

December 11, 2018

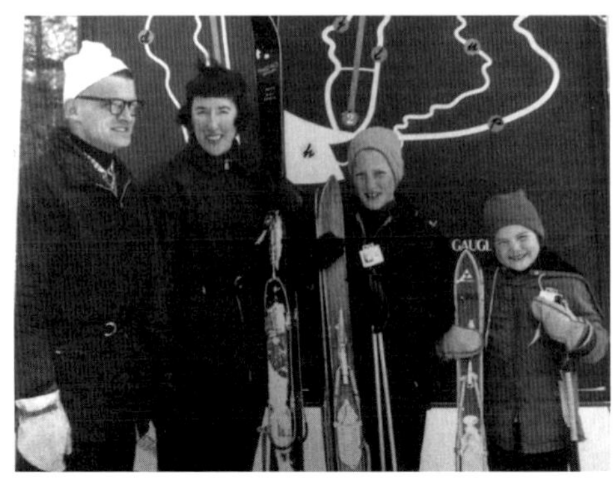

Yesteryear

One wing strong,
the other still healing,
she continues to stretch into
her very own self.
She must have borne the load
on that side—
heaving, sorting, shifting,
trying with all her might.
Plenty has been set down,
but her body
harbored memories
deep within.
She understands now that
releasing and relearning
take time
and she must be patient.
Her highly-trained, analytical side,
so attuned to looking for answers,
needs time to relax
into
being well.
She savors the moments when her
poetic essence shines through,
treasures the recognition that it
has been there all along.
As bitter, stale pains heal,
memories of good times surface.
She pauses in stillness,
sits by the side of her serene lake,
feels even more tension unwind.

A little-girl smile spreads
across her wholesome face.
Yesteryear contained both
heartache and happiness.
As sourness recedes,
she remembers to taste
the sweetness, too.

December 18, 2018

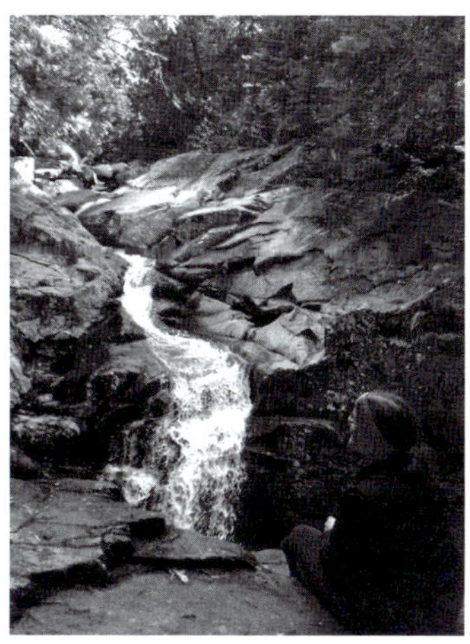

To Be Sure

Slate—the finest-grained metamorphic rock.
It foliates in planes perpendicular to the direction of compression.

Sometimes there is a hollowness to healing,
like some sort of scouring out.
But, at the same time a fullness is present,
or maybe a filling is more accurate.
This emptiness can be fleeting,
or last a while.
No right or wrong—
it happens as you need it to be.
It's as if you become a blank slate,
yet the processes and layers that
formed, fused, cracked,
shifted along the way are still there,
part of your bedrock.
You can access their

energy and history anew,
revisit the wide range
of stories in the layers.
Sometimes a fresh plane emerges,
taking you completely by surprise.
For me it was a fervent missing
of my soulmate as the holidays approach,
followed by the sudden understanding
that I can, in fact,
be whole without him here.
His physical presence, I mean.
Just 18 when our lives merged,
I did not realize how much
I defined my self by our union.
No wonder the aftermath of his death
has taken so long to decipher.
Now I can even more deeply feel
how our time in tandem is
gracefully embedded in my layers
and that my substratum
has long been strong.
My slate is actually quite full,
yet has space for future foliation.
Understandable grief
accompanied by expanding faith.
A Happy Solstice,
to be sure.

December 21, 2018

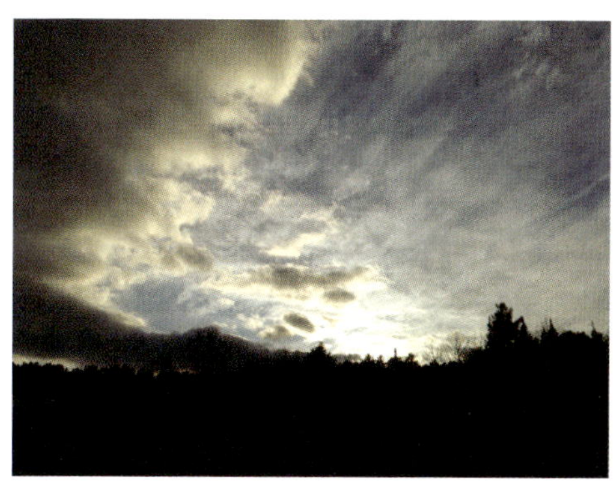

Fully Born

I'm realizing that which was
fully borne by me,
that which should never have been
mine to convey,
has largely been set down for good.
For the good of me, that is.
It was not wrong of me to
lug it for so long.
I simply didn't know any better.
At times anger wends its way into my being
as I more clearly understand the
contents of the satchel
that weighed me down for so long.
Anger for the imposition,
the false sense of ownership,
the absurdity of it all.
But, in the setting down,
the letting go,
there's a distinct feeling of
hmmm ....
I think it's best expressed
as re-birth.
Or, more clearly, a sense of being
fully born.
All the wonderful bits and pieces
that have long been part of me
are adjusting to being
without the weight
of that old, worn satchel.
I feel grateful that

I had the strength to carry it,
found my way to safely
examining its contents,
and now have the opportunity
to drop in
to the newness of being
fully born.

December 31, 2018

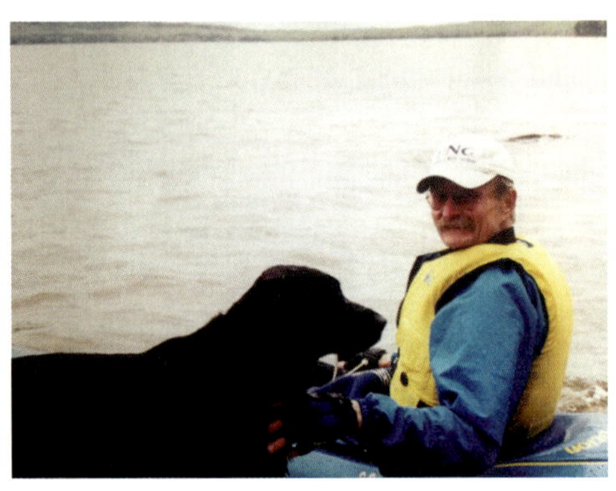

With You and Without You

Dear, dear Barry,
Another New Year's Eve without you.
There are so many
with you
to remember and cherish as those
without you
continue to grow.
I know you know how grateful I am
for the times I shared
with you.
But, you are gone,
have been for quite some time,
and I've had to work hard
to adjust to life
without you.
I know your love remains
a part of my life now.
Recently, though, for the first time

I realized that I can actually be whole
without you.
It seems so simple when I say it aloud,
but actually it has been quite complex
to get to this point.
I was young when we met
and our togetherness
became a cornerstone for me.
I remain grateful for that.
I always will.
But, the time has come for me
to live more fully into my life
without you.
I carry all that we were,
that we had,
tenderly within.
I know your presence,
your support
will show every
now and again.
I'm strong and able,
open and hopeful,
excited about further recovery.
I'm ready to move forward
with you and without you
in a completely singular way.

With so much love,
Sarah
December 31, 2018

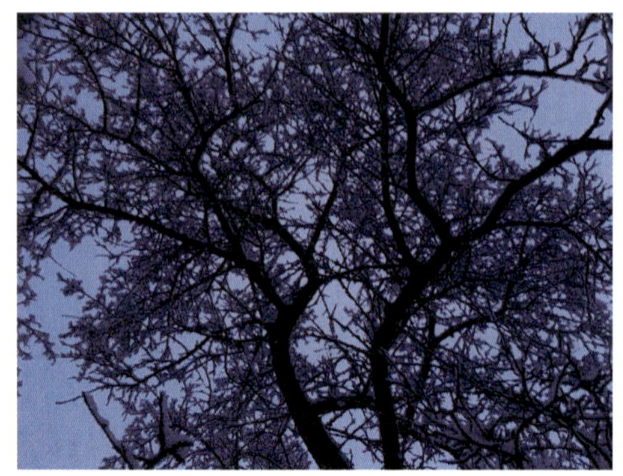

Novelty

A gentle softness arrives
with newness.
New Year, new morning,
new understandings.
Novelty within and without.
Like the freshness of snow
that just happens to blanket the world
in the wee hours
of the first day of the year,
all is muted, quiet, pristine.
For precious moments
stillness can be
seen, heard, felt.
Rain, wind, blue skies
will come and
the beauty will change.
But, right here, right now
there is peace,
a softness to mourning
that, though not sought
or expected,
is gratefully acknowledged.
Breathe deep,
feel the calm,
the scarcity of discomfort.
Celebrate what has come …
novelty.

January 1, 2019

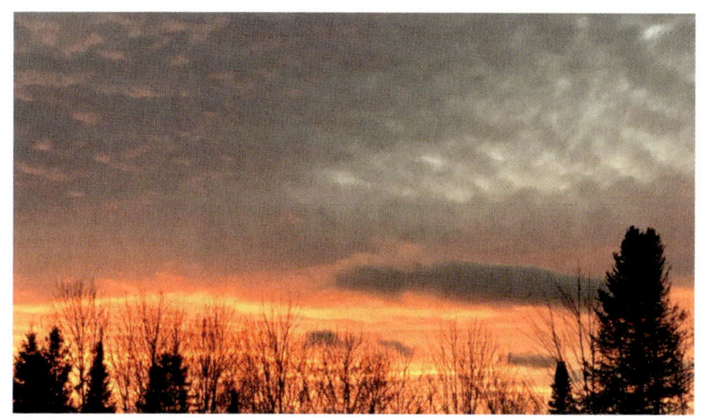

Red Sky at Night

Red sky at night, sailor's delight.
I can hear my father saying that to me
as we watched sunsets
at the lake, in the mountains,
by the sea.
I smile with the memory as I step out
into a winter's eve.
Later, skiing through soft snowy woods,
enchantment flows around and through
my being,
accompanied by a deep awareness
of the power and validity of hope.
It's been there all along for me,
in my heart, my spirit, my words.
Sometimes inner waters
are stirred by winds of change,
though much more gently so.
Old patterns can
still sporadically
cause doubt,
the wonder if I'm wrong.
But the truth is
my craft is as right as can be.
It is safe to
embrace the calm
bob in the waves,
go with the flow.

Red sky at night,
sailor's delight.
Thanks, Dad.
I love you.

January 3, 2019

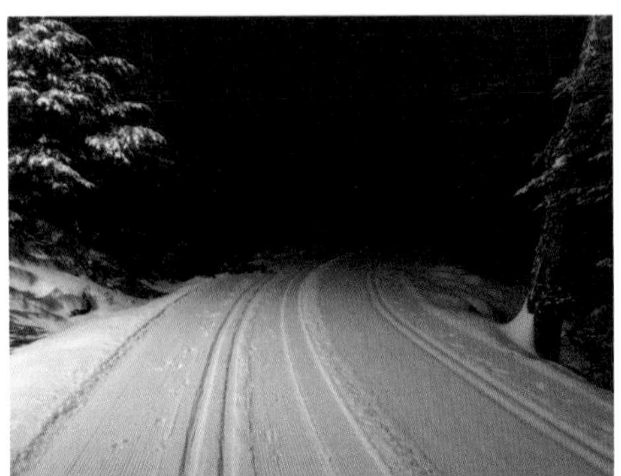

Someone to Cry With

Unexpected, unexpressed emotions
pour forth from previously protected places.
Though unbidden, they must be allowed to flow.
Unfamiliar in their feel,
a product of the newness,
they scour, cleanse, and vitalize.
Lovely little one needs these releases
while she learns not to lug any more,
as does this vibrant, healing me.
But those moments can be
quite a challenge,
for now.
When the waves crest,
there's a craving for
someone to cry with,
who loves me just as I am,
won't push me away
for feeling the deep.
Though there's been no one
in that particular track
for quite some time,
in truth, it's empty,
but not.

I climb a gentle hill,
breathe deep the woodsy air,
listen to the whispers of the wind.
Suddenly that truth washes through me.
I'm never really alone,
though loneliness still visits.
It is safe to freely feel
whatever I do in the moments of my life.
Anyone who judges that is wrong,
not me.
I can be my own
someone to cry with
as more and more I internalize
all that surfaces
from dropping in.

January 9, 2019

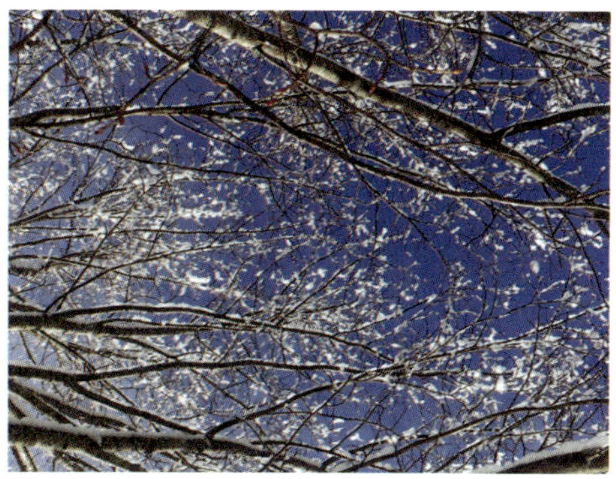

Tears of My Heart

I cried and I cried and I cried.
When I thought I was done
I cried some more.
Tears surfaced
from everywhere at once—
expressions of me,
from me, to me,
for me.
I don't know the origin
of every droplet.
They were an eclectic mix,
a spectrum from sorrow to joy.

I don't know if such a purge
will be repeated.
But if it is,
I will allow.
What emerged that day were
tears of my heart.
Open, cleansing, and
pure.
My feelings freely flowing.
No impediment or judgment.
No fear of rejection or retribution.
Just full on
tears of my heart,
clearing the way even more
to Light, Love,
and exquisite liberty.

January 15, 2019

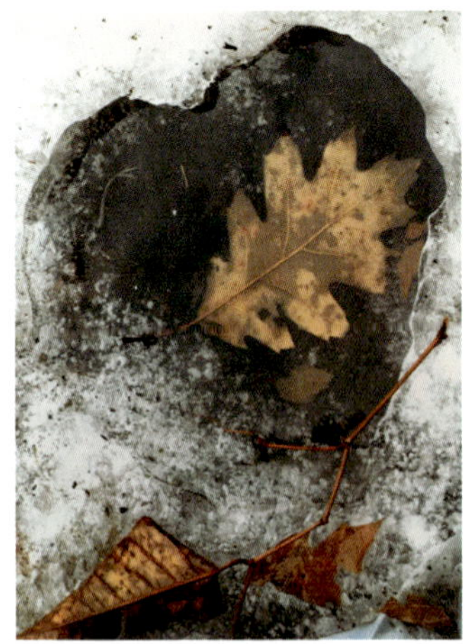

Breathe Deep the Gathering Bloom

Breathe deep the gathering bloom
as visceral freedom oozes, flows
in, out, and all about.
Open-hearted,
she settles more and more and more
into the bounty of exploring
her Divine fathoms.
Gently she twists the lens

and this time,
each time now,
her innate beauty reveals
in such a way
that she simply smiles
and knows.
Some detritus will appear
every now and again,
and there may still be some thawing,
but she is keenly aware
of what to do.
Let the decomposition and melting
kindle
as she roots, foliates,
blossoms.
Ah yes,
breathe deep,
loosen, resolve,
allow the ongoing
graceful unfurling
of her beautiful being.
Breathe deep the gathering bloom.

January 29, 2019

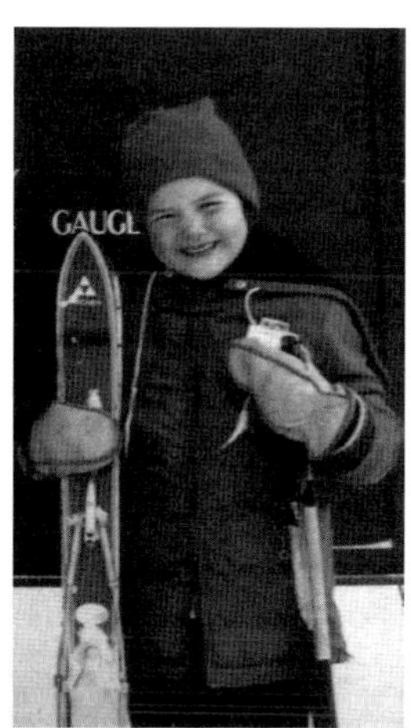

Dear Me,

It's okay.
Feel what you feel,

right here, right now.
It's not wrong, ever.
You've carried the pain of others
long enough.
So long that it was
lodged deep within,
had to be excavated
and explored.
That's why it's been so much work
and the sensations are stale
when they surface and loosen.
Why you feel such a mixture of
frozen and flowy,
confused and clear,
powerless and powerful.
You've done it,
exposed the roots of that
which was imposed.
It's not your pain,
never should have been,
and it's okay to
cry it away,
breathe deep the beauty
of who you are,
let yourself fully unfurl.
You are not hurting anyone,
need not feel beholden
in allowing this to happen.
It's safe and right
and richly deserved
for you to be free
from that particular suffering.
I know it can be scary
and you are still wary of being wrong
when these truths shine through.
That's a tendril of the trauma, though.
You know that now.
It's part of your blossoming to
let it go,
let it flow
away.
Love doesn't hurt,
so let go the pain.

Cry your cleansing tears,
smile your lovely smile,
and be you.

With love from me,
February 12, 2019

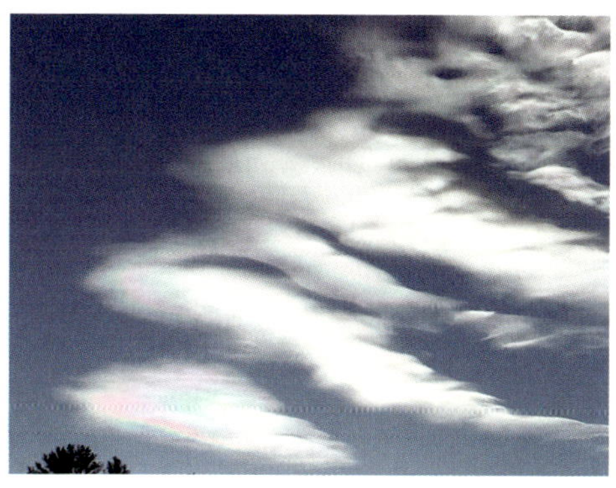

Ethereal Moments

Winter storm lays a blanket of
fluffy, puffy snow
on the sparkling ground.
Three women meet at a trailhead,
two ending their ski,
one just beginning.
A gentle conversation emerges
as they gaze above,
in awe of the way
velvety clouds
stretch and drift,
muted colors gently pulsating
in the layers of droplets.
They talk of love and loss,
grace and gain,
chance and change.
So often it's hard to make sense
of that which happens to us,
around us.
We can get cluttered by
worry and wonder,
care and concern.
And then there are those moments

when you know you are
in the right place,
at the right time.
You can look to the trees
and clouds and waters,
into the eyes of the humans
who share
and let the meaning be
whatever you want it to be.
Ethereal moments of
natural connection
when you can simply
sigh,
settle,
and savor.

February 14, 2019

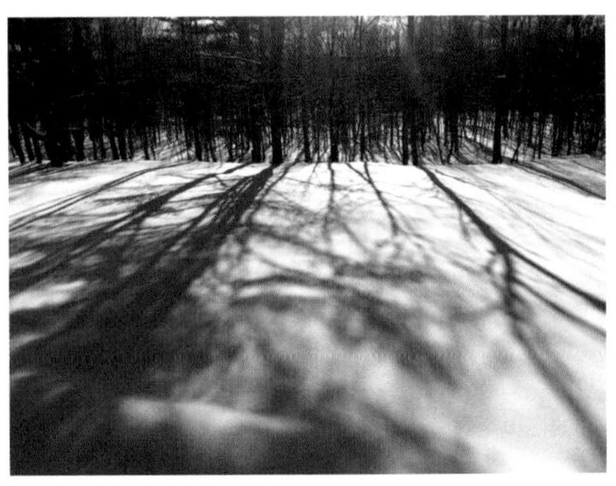

My Best Life Without You

How is it that sometimes I miss you
more than ever before?
A deep missing that involves my
newly breached underpinnings.
Is it because you knew,
you saw those places?
Or maybe it's because I'm older now,
not sure just where
I'm going next.
I don't know if staying in this house
you so loved is good for me.
It's showing its age and needs some repair.

Maybe that's part of the missing, too.
I'm not sure what to do,
how to make the foundation strong again
and deal with the other issues it presents.
I can't seem to keep it warm enough
this winter, either.
Perhaps being cold makes me
feel more alone.
I even wonder if it's because the
world now is just so different,
more troubling.
At times things are so clear and
I feel like I just know.
You died,
I'm still here.
I have intrepidly explored, adjusted,
grown stronger and wiser even.
Then there are those ambiguous times
where I feel murky and unsure.
The juxtaposition of the two
makes me feel tired all the way
down to the depths of my soul.
I don't experience it as good or bad,
just challenging and true,
part of the whole picture—
both close to home
and in the wider world.
I miss the sense of being in tandem
as we dealt with whatever came our way.
Soulmates we were, are.
So, that must be it.
I can finally be at peace
with missing you with my entire being.
I imagine in doing that
I can more heartily live
my best life without you.

February 19, 2019

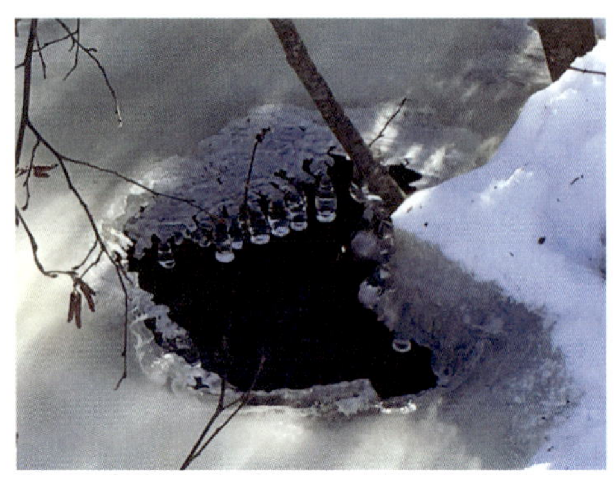

Love You Still

Dear sweet Sarah T.,
I'm here and I
love you still.
I am in awe of all you have done
since I died,
though I'm not surprised in the least.
Your courage and grit,
combined with such gentle compassion,
are part of what drew me to you
along the shores of Saddleback Lake
during that magical summer of 1975.
I saw it, felt it in the
twinkle of your eyes,
set of your chin,
warmth of your smile,
rhythm of your words.
It was in the way you
pounded tennis balls,
carved a turn,
mothered our children,
loved them and me.
We had a good run
you and I,
but because I left when I did,
how I did,
you've had to work hard to recover.
You barely had time to grieve
as so many challenges
and changes happened at once.
I know it's part of you to be a giver.

But, now you know
it's also good and right to receive.
So yes, sweet Sarah, go on and
breathe deep the gathering bloom.
Do that not once,
but over and over and over again.
Do what you need to do
in any way that you choose.
It really is okay.
Feel what you feel—
little you, big you,
every space and place within.
Thaw, flow, rest, and recoup.
Honor your graceful gems, allow them
to glisten and gleam in the light of day.
Feel the joys of being you and
always, always remember that I
love you still,
Barry Q. Carlson

February 20, 2019

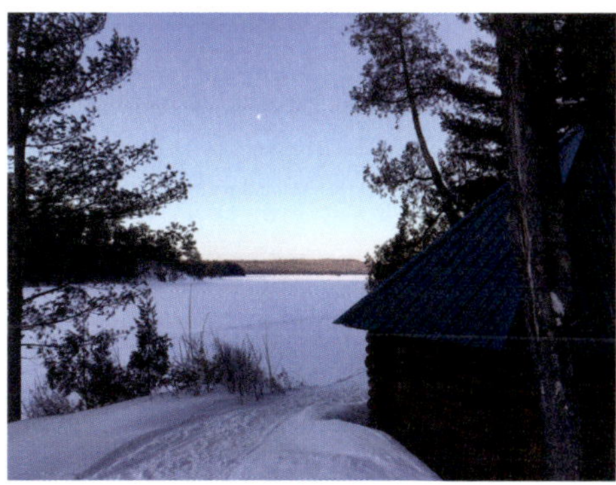

Reminder From a Winter Sky

Octagonal cabin sits by
quiet, frozen waters.
Sun slips behind a tranquil horizon
as friends gather together
in a temporary home.
Conversations ebb and flow,
like the ongoing movement beneath the ice.
Laughter, connection, depth and delight

course in and around the lively group
as life stories merge and mingle.
Stars and moon
saturate the darkening sky,
weary skiers rejuvenate and rest.
Night dwindles, morning expands.
Waning moon slowly recedes
as sunlight bathes the opposite shore.
Humans awaken to a brand new day,
ready for another ski adventure
with ample opportunities
to breathe the forest air,
soak in the warmth of the sun,
stretch physical limits.

This skier ponders the way the moon
waxes and wanes
as her energy does the same
on the ski out.
Without one there would not be the other,
and there is beauty in all the phases.
She knows to simply allow her fatigue
and be thankful for her hardiness within.
With that comes a sense of accomplishment,
a freshening of spirit,
and her stride strengthens once again.
Such a lovely reminder from a winter sky—
just as night gives way to morning,
so does waning lead to
novelty, growth, and fullness.

February 24, 2019

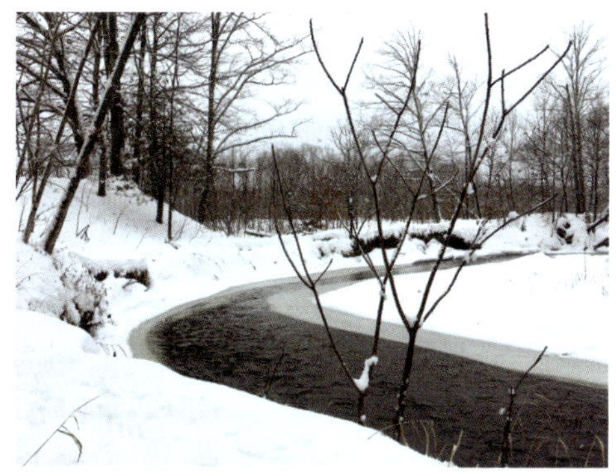

Onward We Flow

As things open and a new flow ensues
there can be a gentle discomfort,
a feeling of tender vulnerability.
It's about a shift away from susceptibility
to that which used to cause hurt.
Emergence and conclusion happening,
sometimes separately,
but more often at once.
A sense of disturbance
may be present,
but is accompanied by
a flourishing appreciation of self
and a differentiation from difficulties.
You realize that problems are not of you,
do not define you,
and there's a lovely freedom to
choose how and when to react.
This notion is deeply empowering and,
for one who is used to being hurt,
takes some time for adjustment.
Deeper and stronger, though,
is a continually expanding sense
of no longer being victimized,
of trusting in who you are
in any given moment.
Unease, insight, and freedom
often travel together,
especially when you
welcome them aboard.

So, like burbling water
in the depth of winter,
onward we flow
together.

February 26, 2019

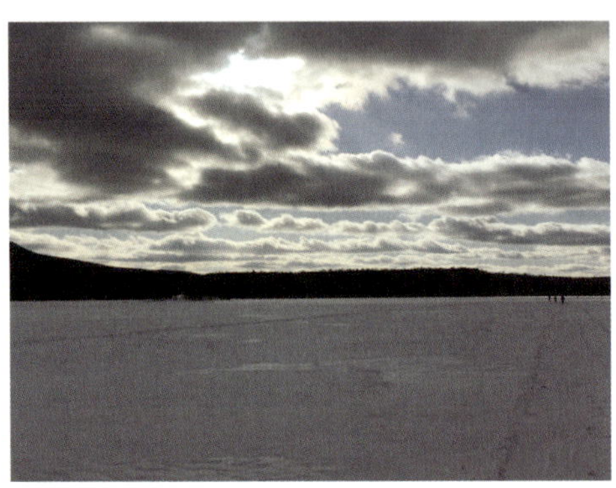

The Power of Quiet

There's a quiet to being a widow
that is like no other.
At times it involves a deep craving
to share life experiences with
the one who knew you the best.
I believe in continued connection
and I treasure those times when
his love shines through.
Whether a sighting in nature,
words that wend through my mind and onto paper,
or simply a sensation beyond explanation,
I do know he's still there.
Through my writing I talk and process and heal.
I didn't mean for this to happen.
It just did.
Recently I realized that without the aspect of stillness
poems such as this would not have come to be.
This understanding is so important for my process
because usually there is very little talking back.
I put some of my musings out into the world
and, for the most part,
don't really know where they go
or what effect they have.

I found that confusing for a time,
but now I can view it as similar
to stopping in my tracks
during a ski on a frozen lake
to breathe and be.
I was alone, but not.
All was still, but not.
There was silence, but not.
Friends skied ahead or rested in cabins.
Clouds drifted overhead, water moved beneath my feet.
My steady breath and the constant breeze
synchronized into a symphony.
Though responses are always welcome,
yearnings and loneliness will still visit,
I can honestly say that I'm grateful
for the power of quiet.

February 27, 2019

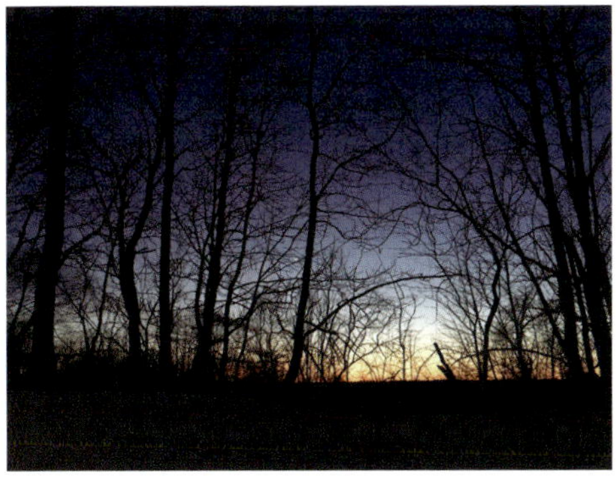

Confluence

Wispy, pink and mauve clouds drift soundlessly
across an early March sky.
Dusk approaches as more vibrant colors
spread across the horizon.
Waxing crescent moon seems to follow the sun
in the ongoing interplay of celestial bodies.
Banks of snow appear solid,
though they shift and settle with
temperature fluctuations
of longer, brighter days.
Stoic, sleepy trees stand ready

for sap to flow
with awakening.
Warm-hearted woman
takes a moment
to gaze upward
and inward,
smiling at the confluence
of completion,
emergence,
continuous phases,
and the ever-present promise of
new beginnings.

March 9, 2019

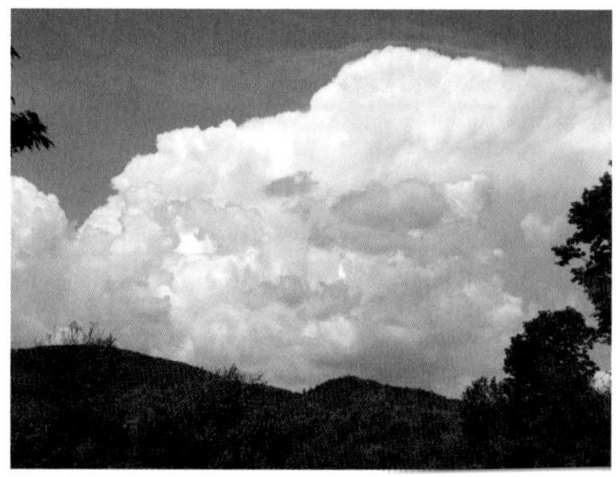

A Perfect Storm

Some things are simply futile.
There's literally nothing one can do.
And, yet, there's a sense of constant demand.
Try this, fix that, come to the rescue.
But you can't fix someone else's brokenness,
or rescue them from being stuck in their own muck.
And you shouldn't be expected to.
However, that can be part of the challenge.
You've been groomed to try and try
and try again,
no matter what.
You are yanked this way and that,
trapped in the midst of irrational forces.
One day, though, you begin to realize
that you don't have to yield to their energy

any longer
and you slowly,
bit by bit,
claim your freedom.
It may be that one day,
when you're in a place of healing,
those forces converge
for a perfect storm.
Multiple fronts crash into each other and,
though you thought you had already
given voice to the distress,
your body simply needs to express.
You ride the storm surge,
tossed this way and that,
eventually emerging to calmer waters.
It's a struggle to pull away from the trappings
and come back,
but you do.
It may not feel like quite the same place
and you are stronger, wiser, so much more free.
Queasy and a bit off balance,
you orient more distinctly to the truth of you,
your place in the world.
You trust that the residual
pitching and rolling will settle,
the pressures that precipitated
a perfect storm will separate and dissipate
as they blow farther and farther away.
It begins to dawn on you
that you are actually rescuing yourself.
Though gently unsettled,
you feel buoyant, secure, and right.

March 12, 2019

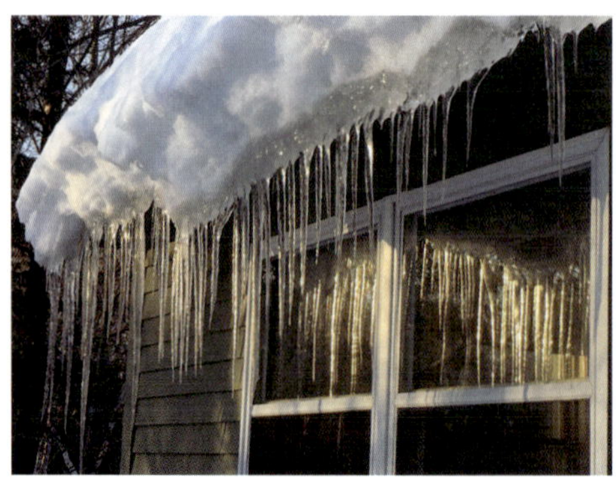

Quickthaw

Complex system of sculptured ice,
glacial in nature,
caused by pressures and shifts,
floes and fissures—
moored deep, deep within
a genuinely warm-hearted being.
Though thawing has been part of her process,
one day faultless conditions clear the way for
a quickthaw.
A flash flood follows
with truly torrential emotions
busting loose her banks.
She is there, in it,
at the same time an observer,
marveling at the beauty
of diverging flows.
She experiences a curious sense of safety,
a distinct ability to be with it, without it,
profit from its power.
Secure in her vessel that,
though tossed about,
stays the course,
is steadfast and right.
And, then …
things settle into a slow and steady melt,
a sliding into newness yet again,
residue dripping away with gentle abandon.
That which remains rearranges to find its rightful place
as she dwells in Light, swells with Love.
Familiar kaleidoscope effect with

an energy that is novel and needed
as her lens becomes more and more clear.
This quickthaw has a power
that once may have made her fearful,
but now she can embrace
for the healing it produces,
the hope it fosters,
the truth it sets free.

March 25, 2019

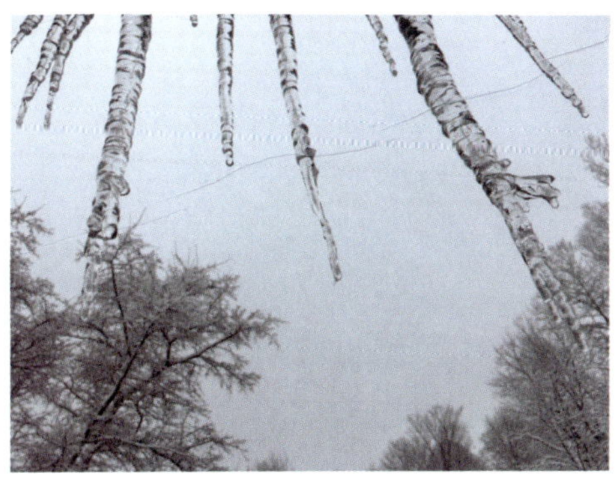

The Poetry of Stillness

Reflective, seemingly placid waters
are actually on the move.
A natural glide whenever, wherever
there is a slope, however slight.
Motion caused by that downhill flow,
temperature fluctuations,
underground springs,
gentle breezes,
fish swimming,
or even a human paddling,
is always present.
The hush of a sunset,
hope of a sunrise,
pull of the moon,
lull of the wind
without movement would not be.
Like the subtle drip of icicles
on a muted morning
after a spring storm,

there are times
when all seems paused
and there's a clarity to the interplay
of dark and light,
to what one sees, feels, comprehends
that is deeply undeniable.
All just is as it is,
a poetically pure moment
of truth and stillness.

April 10, 2019

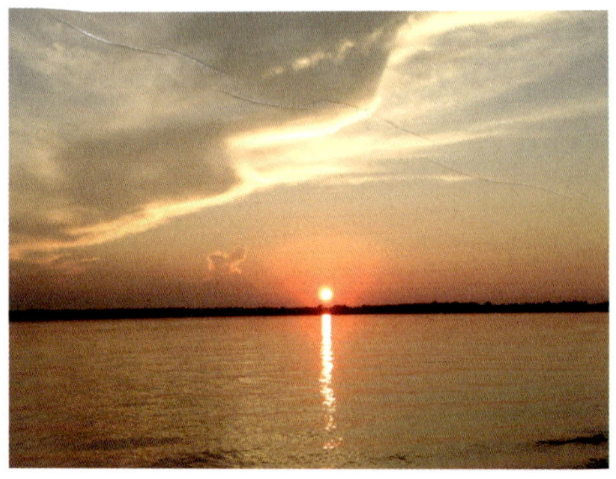

The Health of Hush

Winds of change swirl and surge,
blow in, around, and through.
In the lull that follows one can breathe,
appreciate calm, let things reorient.
Ever more subtle,
the pull of the moon moves oceans,
tides rise and fall
with in-between moments of
noticeable balance.
Each morning,
if conditions are right,
one can witness our star seem to rise.
With it comes the hope of all
that could dawn.
Time marches on,
twilight approaches,
sun slips behind hills, trees,
or a wide-open horizon.

There's a stretch of hush
as light transitions to night.
A deep sense of vigor crystallizes
in the lulls, pulls, hope,
and hush of healing.
Stillness allows for movement—
radiance steadily brightens
as a whole being
settles into the warmth
of genuine love,
smiles with
gentle gratitude
for the flowing, knowing,
and glowing
of the health of hush.

April 23, 2019

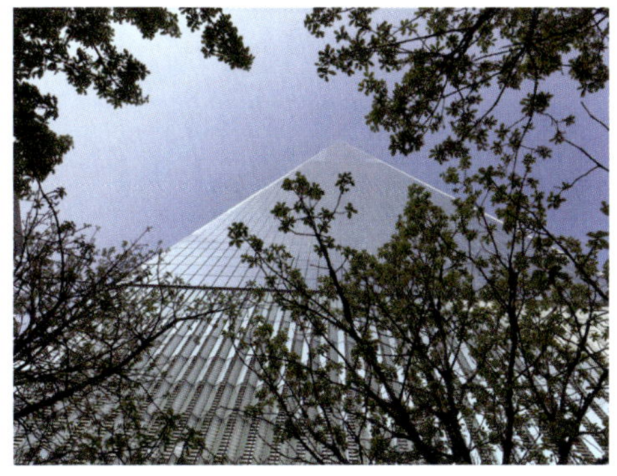

Rise Up

Brokenness
and the accompanying trauma
are part of living
on this planet.
While some tragedies are shared,
each human has their unique story.
Reasons known or not,
effects tangible or difficult to discern,
our narratives are complex
and contain heartache.
Inner reflection,
the exploration of

deep, achy places
requires courage,
determination,
and honesty.
Within the rubble
is the tenacity of the human spirit,
a collective wish for peace,
the goodness and purity of recovery.
We can and do
rise up
again and again and again.
At times this is hugely visible,
like a towering structure
that seems to stretch
to the heavens above.
Other times it's as subtle
as the shared joy of thousands
of like-minded people
pedaling in the same direction
on a rainy May day
in a city
where resilience,
rebuilding,
and renewal
are conspicuous, visceral, and true.

May 8, 2019

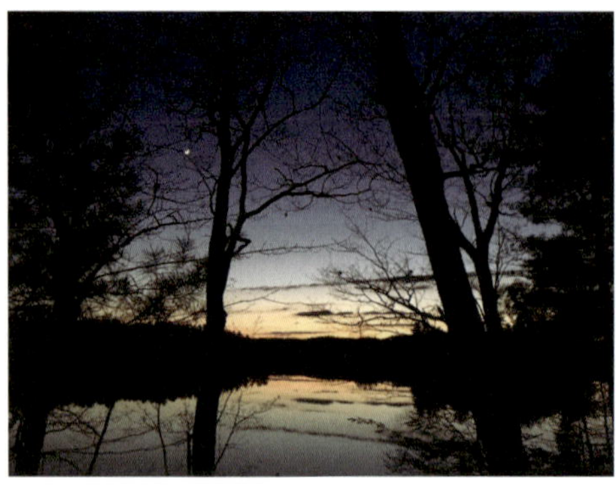

Still Waters

Lay back,
absorb all that has come

from your exploration.
Relax as you let still waters
support you, caress you,
gently transport you
to pristine places.
Your revelations of the goodness,
pureness,
beauty that is you
can and will expand even more.
New challenges,
some that may be furtherings
of what you thought had resolved,
will present themselves.
That's life as a caring, feeling,
healing human.
It might be confusing as
your newfound sense of health
converges with brokenness.
But you've dealt
with cross currents before,
though maybe not quite as strong.
You're fine.
So, lay back and sink in,
safe in the knowledge that
still waters
do run deep.
And it's from the stillness
that your wonderful wild child
allows her being
to fully immerse in
universal Love
as she beams
and thrives.

May 21, 2019

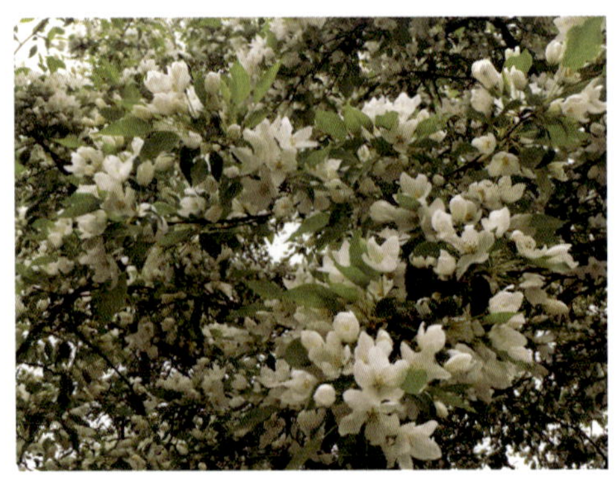

May 29th

I've had such a
flurry of feelings
today.
That's not unusual
since today is the last day of
'weird week',
which always concludes on this date.
Two birthdays, two death days
come and gone
again,
all while school is winding up
before the slide
into summer.
But, today seemed sort of magnified
with a range of echoing emotions
that swayed and swirled within.
It wasn't bad or good,
right or wrong.
I just felt what was there
without a pull to fully understand
why or how or if.
It's a Wednesday again,
only the second time since 2002.
That likely had something to do
with it, too.
Body memories
are so strong
and wise.
May 29th,
you seem to be ending with

feelings of gratitude and
accomplishment,
combined with a healthy dose of
sorrow and fatigue.
Good night,
and thank you.
I'll feel you again
next year.

May 29, 2019

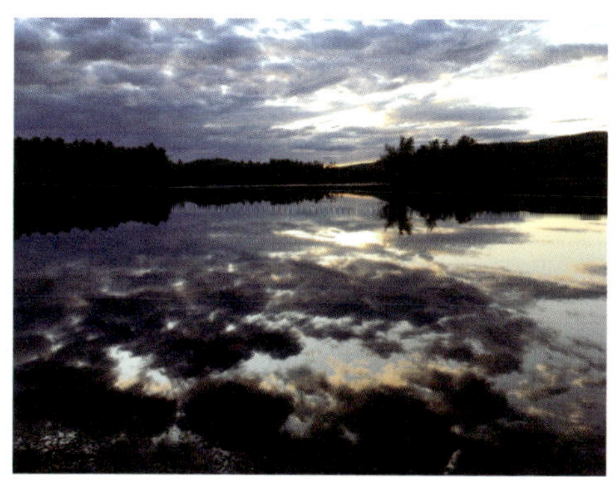

Regard, Reflect, and Receive

Somber clouds surround.
Intrepid traveler ponders, wonders,
but does not worry.
She trusts that she is heading
in the right direction,
though darkness is present.
Her body slowly relaxes and
she notices a golden glimmer ahead.
Wonder slips into awe as
she transitions into the glow.
She glances left to the setting sun,
then right to the arch of a rainbow
that straddles the horizon.
Contemplating recent releases,
she smiles at the timely message from
the omnipresent sky.
Over and over and over again
sky talk makes sense.
Dark, light, shades of gray,

silver linings, radiance.
Constant motion combined
with peace and quiet.
All there for the eye to behold
once time is taken to notice.
And, if one is troubled,
unsure, or weary
it is vital to
regard, reflect,
and receive.

June 21, 2019

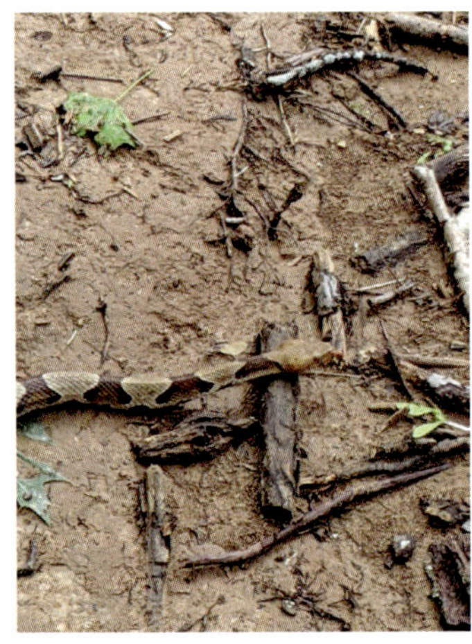

Lesson From a Southern Snake

Fear is something that is precise, concrete.
It's there for a distinct reason—
that being protection.
A snake on a trail
in an unfamiliar place produces fear,
at least in me.
I knew to be wary as we walked along.
Warm climate, wet conditions
had my well-learned hyper-vigilance activated.
And there it was
right in the trail,
though deeply disguised.
I may have sensed it before seeing it
as I called out in alarm.

My fellow hiker turned back
and once we realized we were safe,
that the snake showed no inkling to strike,
fear shifted to awe.
It was actually quite beautiful as it
slowly slithered into a pile of detritus
left behind by the previous night's rain.
There were clear boundaries
as we respected its space,
and it ours.

Then there are shapeless things that
cause anxiety.
Relationships that do not have
understandable borders.
Erroneous beliefs
imposed by outside forces
during tender life phases.
Those who have no desire to
explore, discover, change.
As one heals, it becomes more clear
the difference between anxiety and fear.
Fear can serve an important purpose
in the right conditions.
Anxiety, though nebulous,
can be acknowledged
and released
as one assimilates, brightens,
trusts the pure and benign
power of Love.

June 21, 2019

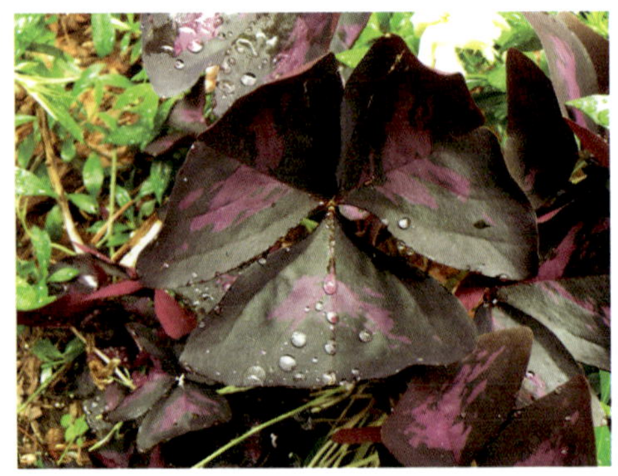

When We Were Four

Our family—
mother, father, son, daughter.
For more than 17 years
we were four.
So much love—
betwixt and between,
through the joys and challenges
of growing up,
living life.
But one spring day,
in an instant,
we became three.
Everything we knew felt askew,
yet onward we went
each rearranging our pieces
in our own ways,
in our own time.
Emotions surface and show,
or get bundled up and put away
for another time.
Neither right nor wrong,
we've done the best we can
along the way
as we readjust and reorient,
uncover the radiance in change.
Though we did
suddenly become three
on that day so long ago,
there's a curative, bountiful power

in remembering the love
that we shared
when we were four.

June 24, 2019

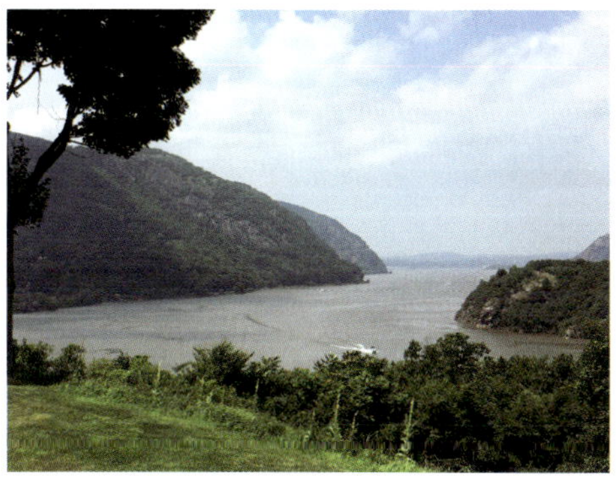

Messages of Silence

On the edge of the Hudson—
emergence of connection,
then silence.
Sit, walk, feel, eat, sleep … repeat.
Individual tears of heartache, sorrow,
joy, revelation.
Together, yet separate,
each person's inner adventure unique.
This human, this poet
experiences deep grief
from sources known, sources not.
In honoring that, sitting with it,
there emerges a more clear
sense of strength, sureness, wisdom,
accomplishment, health.
Beyond words and sounds
one accesses the essence
of insight, belonging,
peace, love.
A sensation that,
though boundless,
eventually feels safe and secure
in a most fluid way.
Currents ebb and flow

in whatever direction is necessary
for that person at that time.
Inner radiance pulsates
with the veracity of awareness
as the promise of
an undefined, yet palpable
community begins to form.
The banks determine
the course of a river,
but waters within
find their own way,
in their own time,
mingling with that
which is true and right.
Such are the messages of silence.

July 8, 2019

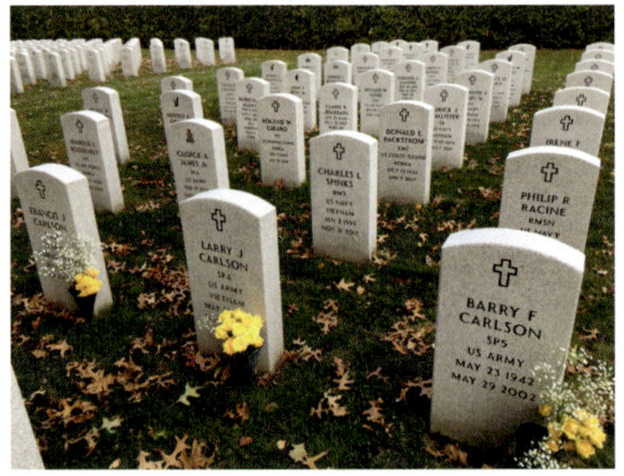

Messages of a Different Silence

It's been so long since we've talked.
You visit in my dreams,
in natural connections,
in the energy of love continued.
But, you are always quiet.
It's up to me
to notice, define, embrace.
Your brother had a wish
that you and he and your dad
be honored and rest together.
I had given him some of your ashes,
though the rest remain with me.

So, for the first time since you died,
I see a singular gravestone
with your name on it.
It's in a place that is unfamiliar to me,
but there it is, you are.
At first it is surreal,
especially coming on the heels
of processing multifaceted grief
at a retreat in silence.
As I stand there with your sister
and let the sensations sink in,
I feel the love of a father
and twin brothers
who served our country,
graced our family
in diverse ways
for so many years.
I am awash in
gratitude, pride,
relationship,
and healthy sorrow.
Messages of a
very different,
though just as powerful,
silence.

July 10, 2019

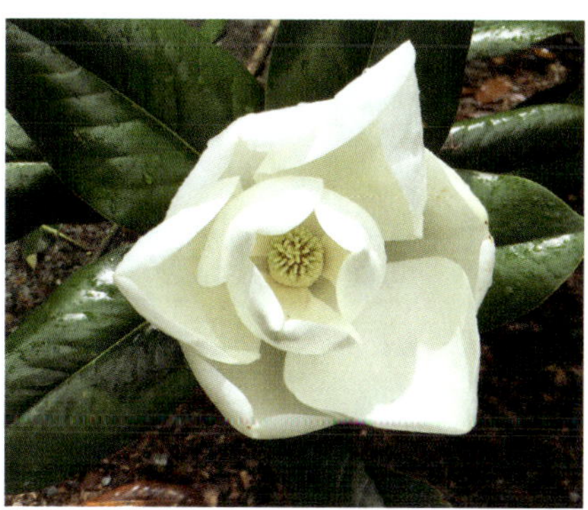

See Me?

Adorable toddler lurches across the grass asking,
"See me? See me, Mommy?"

His mother smiles, knowing
that her child wants to be in her arms.
And she wants that child in hers
just as much.
She picks him up and his body
seems to melt into hers
as mother love, child love
converge into
tender moments of togetherness.
She sees him in a most deep
and loving way,
knows he sees her
seeing him.
Time passes,
challenges come,
heartache happens.
Mother love stays strong,
though not as easily merged.
She sees him still, the two of them,
now adults, both.
The sense of being unseen, though,
stirs around within
and she realizes it stems
from bygone years and
her own grief.
Now inner wisdom
helps her understand that
though she might feel, or actually be,
unseen in some situations
it does not mean she is not there.
What's important is that she see
and experience her
very own self
right here, right now.
See me?
Yes, I most definitely do,
my love.
I see you.
Do you see me seeing you?

July 10, 2019

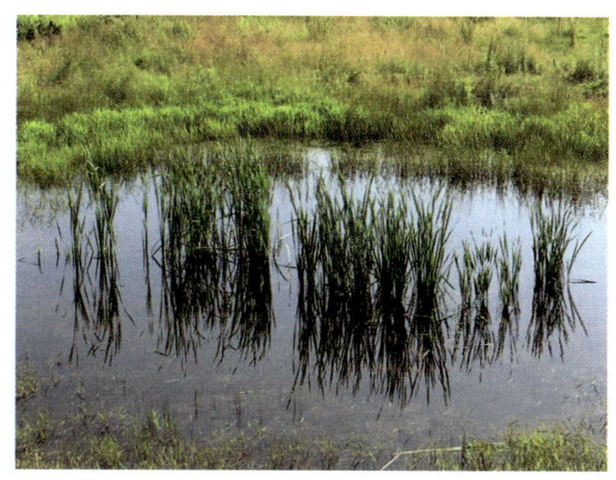

Believe

Inner wisdom softly speaks
with a reminder to trust
those spaces and places
where knowing resides.
Even when things feel stuck
and pain is strong.
Even when you swirl
with things untamed, unnamed.
Even when those spiky spots
need a voice.
Continue to pause, breathe,
acknowledge.
Keep honoring the seeds
that have been sown
on your journey towards
unconditional Love
experienced unconditionally.
Let them sprout, grow, blossom
in their own way,
in their own time,
as they have and will.
You know
when to wander and wonder,
soothe and saturate,
accept and allow.
You aren't unseen
if you see your own
wonderful and unique self.
Believe all the way

in that Love,
in this you.
Just do it …
believe.

July 17, 2019

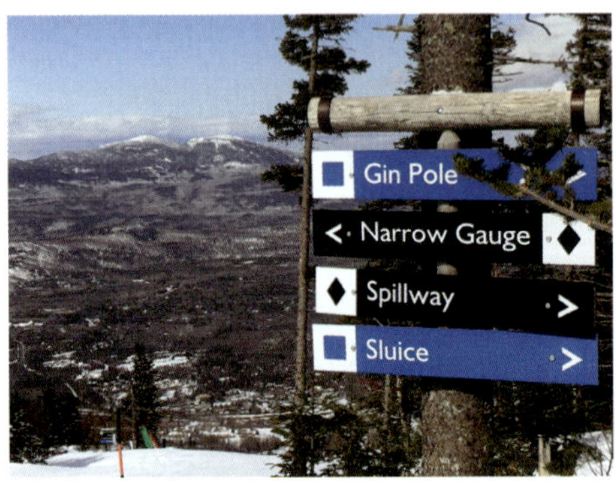

The Gifts That Nestle Within

Sturdy, athletic, vibrant—
she lays her skis on edge,
carves graceful arcs
in the freshly groomed snow.
She loves this trail for its openness,
precise fall lines,
the possibility that someone
might notice her skill and talent.
At the very same time
there trickles within her body
wariness, worry, foreboding.
Does she still need to fend off, protect,
or is it safe to fully let go, let flow?
The unease is slight,
feels musty,
but is clearly present.
She stops and gazes over
the valley of her youth.
Breathing in the cool, crisp mountain air
she honors what was,
feels the tenseness
of those deep, dank places
soften yet again,

smiles with appreciation of the shift.
Body, mind, spirit slowly and gently
continue to settle into
a less impeded flow,
a crystallizing recognition
of the gifts that nestle within
and the gentleness with which
she allows them out into
the light of day.
Spirit free, heart full, mind settled,
she gives a slight push,
glides down the slope,
delights in the rhythms
of her singular mountain dance.

July 26, 2019

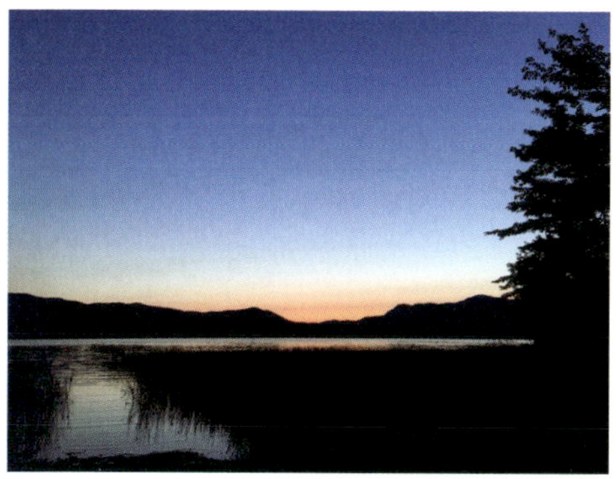

Happy to Be

On the one hand
pain, embarrassment, unease.
On the other
vigor, peace, liberty.
The first will happen
from time to time,
but need not be the norm.
The second can and should be
accessed, allowed, honored,
will aid in the continued lessening
of once powerful, troubling currents.
The being in the middle of it all
more and more trusts

the efficacy and validity
of her travels.
When she tumbles,
she gets back up,
checks in,
asks for help when needed.
She relishes the times when she can
sink further into her being,
relax by a shore,
enjoy the calm energy
of mountains, waters, sky.
In those moments she feels
settled and sure,
radiant and right,
full and free.
She is
happy to be
in the daunting,
daring,
definite
delicate,
divine
moments of her life.

July 29, 2019

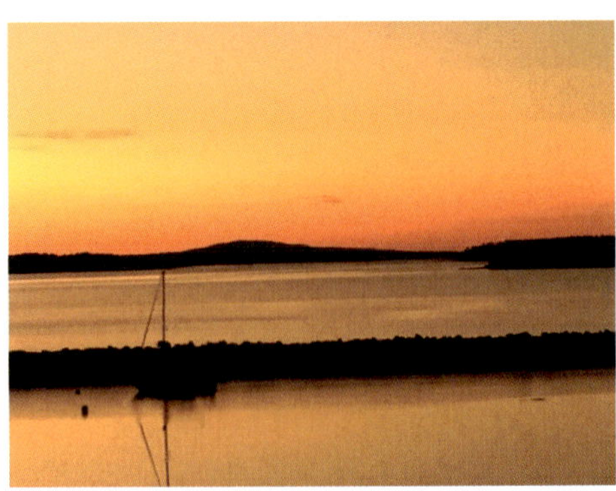

In the Stillness

Ever so slowly sunlight widens
as night gives way to morning.
Though birds do chitter
and soft breezes stir,

there's a serene quiet
to those moments of transition
as human rhythms thrum.
Keen mind settles,
gentle heart pulsates,
breath comes easily.
As she wakens and reflects,
she notices
a deeper sense of immersion.
In the activity of
sharing stories
with new people,
pedaling long distances
on unfamiliar roads,
letting go of a
need to hold back
or keep up,
a novel aspect of calm presents.
In the stillness
there exists an ever more
vivid, dynamic, limitless
sense of being.

August 11, 2019

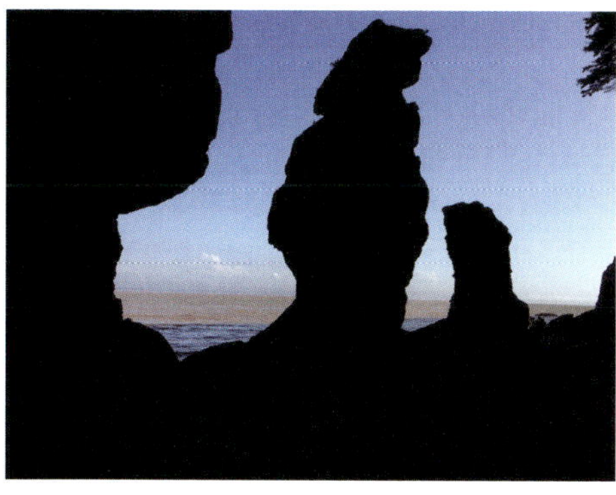

Incoming Tides

Strong and solid she stands,
despite diverse forces that
once threatened her core.
A near constant barrage of things that,
looking back,

she understands were not of her
or about her.
However, they did
create discord where
harmony should have been.
More and more she internalizes
that those days are over,
need not injure her any further.
She can almost see herself
as a miracle of survival
when her rhythms hum
with lively abandon—
like waves rolling
onto a sandy beach,
water dispersing to wherever
it needs to go.
It is her health,
the beam of her inner truth,
that leads the way,
has all along.
More and more she feels its warmth,
can bask in its vitality,
comprehends its boundless nature.
She experiences the effect
of her genuine presence
both within herself and on others,
relaxes ever more deeply
into her being
as sediments stir and settle
with incoming tides
of assurance, peace, awareness,
and Love.

August 12, 2019

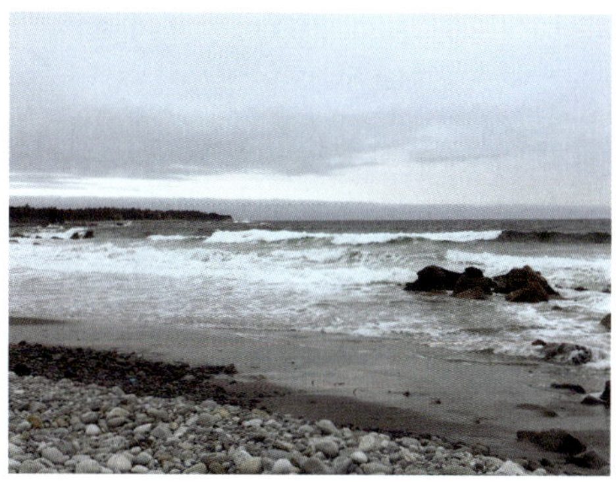

Right There, Right Then

Low fog lessens over the horizon
as waves swell, crest, roll—
again and again and again.
A mesmerizing cadence
that gently transfixes
those who sit and settle
on the rocky beach.
Seaweed sways back and forth,
accompanied by the sumptuous sound
of salty liquid lapping onto land.
Feet sink into soft sand
as body eases,
mind lulls,
spirit widens.
Breath moves with shared energy
as ocean rhythms meld
with inner tempos.
Nothing to do
but be
right there,
right then.

August 19, 2019

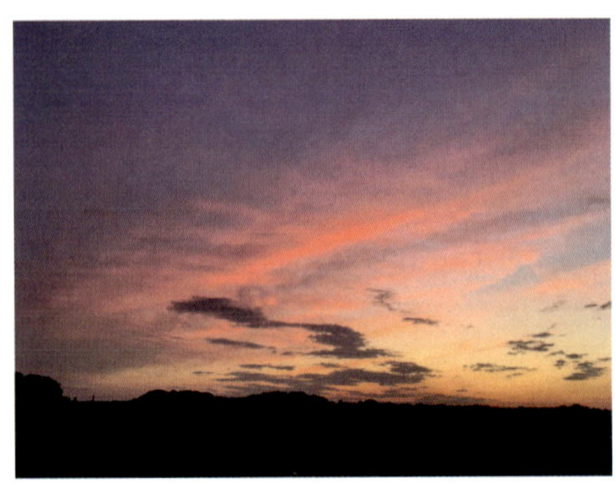

Nice in Here

I feel as if I'm moving
all the way in.
Like some places were off limits before,
or maybe were taken up by things
recently vacated.
Either way, I love the sensation
of filling in my own far reaches.
When it happens I access more keenly
that boundless expanse
I once thought did not include me.
I have a limitless, unencumbered
sense of being,
a now-ness that seamlessly blends
wild child wonder
with poetic wisdom.
These words don't really do justice
to what these feelings are like.
In fact,
as I watch my pencil
slide across the page of my journal,
hand illuminated by the evening sun,
it's almost as if I don't know
who is doing the writing,
though the described sensations
are strong and true.
Not a dissociation at all,
but more like a re-association
as my tender tones
settle into a sweet and steady harmony.
Simply a delightful newness of

my experience of me.
I like it
and I'm finding
that it's really quite
nice in here.

August 27, 2019

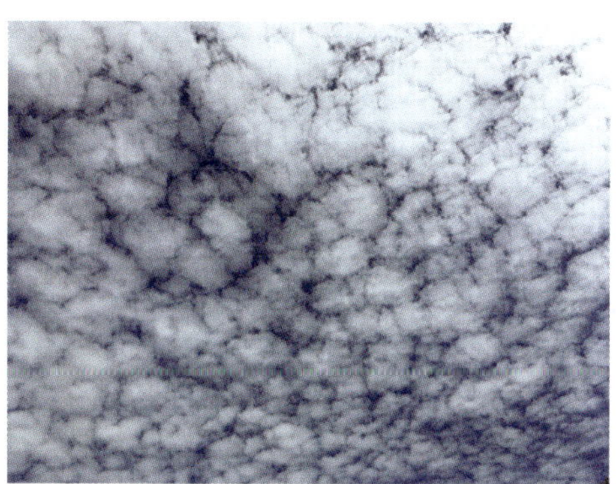

In the Currents of Now

By the shore of her serene lake
she dips her toes in the water.
With a gentle sigh
she decides to slide all the way in.
Relaxing in the beauty of
her inner landscape,
her vibrant smile reflects
how nice it truly is within.
At the very same time
deep, stale sorrows swirl
with an energy mostly of release,
not threat,
though sometimes it is still
hard for her to tell the difference.
She learns to find solace
in not always understanding
the source or the meaning
of that which goes.
More and more at ease
with whatever is there,
she lets go the urge to
remember, relive, rerun

distressing scenes of the past.
She encourages her own self
to trust her healing
without trying so hard,
caring too much.
Deep weariness washes away,
replaced by even deeper comfort.
Turning her gaze to the sky above
she feels those stories of so very long ago,
the ones that had her believing
inherent wrongness,
lose their veracity and ferocity.
Her body slackens as a refreshing faith
that feels both foreign and familiar
saturates and revives.
Softly, slowly it dawns on her
that maybe,
just maybe,
she can consider herself
a conduit
to and from the Divine.
The mutuality, relationship
she has been craving
is right there, right here.
Hopeful, she lays back
and floats more fully
in the currents of now.

September 12, 2019

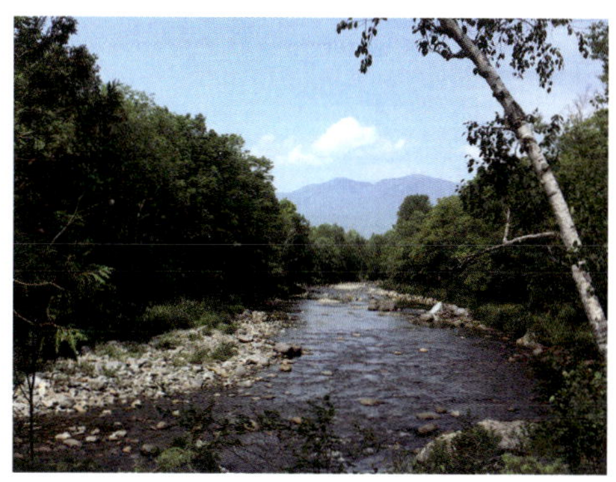

Gather

I carried it for so long,
though I don't really have words
that properly convey
I know it to be gloomy, tangly, once mighty.
I long thought it was stronger than me.
But the antithesis is true.
I am stronger, have always been.
I had to acknowledge it,
explore it for a time,
learn from it
so I could welcome faith
in the currents of now.
Along the way I kept thinking
I had it figured out,
could set it down and move on.
I'd relax in the flow
and then it would slither in
from an unnoticed direction,
implore me to pay attention
just when I felt full and free.
So recently, from a place of safety,
I reluctantly listened yet again.
I felt confined by it and distinct from it.
I felt exasperation toward it
and compassion for me.
I felt stale constriction
and hinting liberation.
Though I tried to waylay them,
tears demanded my attention.
Now, as underlying,

unneeded intensity lessens,
I can absorb that I am truly okay,
have the ability to let the muck filter away.
I belong, I am safe, I can trust.
I can believe in mutuality
with the Divine without fear.
Whatever fear attached to that
simply is not mine,
has no meaning for me.
With fondness for self,
gratitude for growth,
recognition of radiance,
I softly, tenderly reorient and release.
There may be bits that straggle, or not.
It doesn't really matter because
they will fall away
at the opportune time.
I am free to lovingly lighten up,
gather what this meander reveals.

September 15-22, 2019

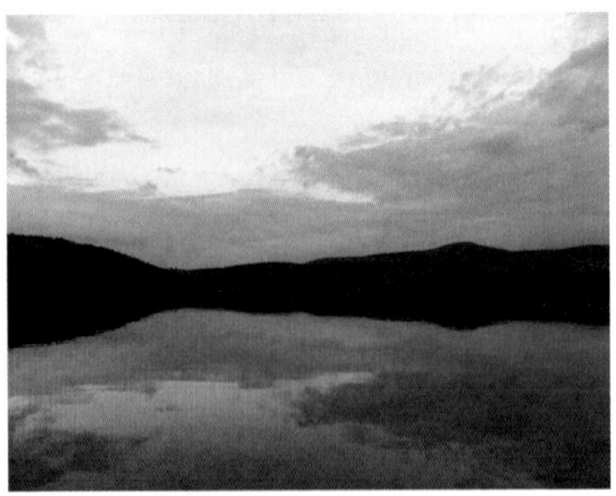

Divine Comfort

An imposed sense of being unseen,
unheard, unsure within,
fabricated by
a slow, shady smothering,
had long been her covert companion.
Uncharted exploration
uncovers the warp and weft of
love and truth,

enables distinction to spread.
Vulnerability remains present
as she continues her travels.
Sliding through silky waters,
liquid caresses each pore,
wraps her in the softness
of contentment.
Solid shores surround,
pure fluid supports,
genial clouds hover.
Suddenly rain begins to fall
on the tranquil surface
as dancing ripples widen,
inverted droplets cavort
in a show of celestial grandeur.
She beams and giggles
as the majesty of the
unexpected moment permeates.
Rain subsides, sun peeks,
swimmer settles.
In the stillness
she recognizes the remedy
for that which was inflicted
and took hold before
she knew any better.
She lays back,
finds the courage to more deeply
dispel antiquated guidance,
feel the freedom of her flow,
allow Divine comfort to
enfold and enliven as it
gently weaves its way into her fabric.

October 7, 2019

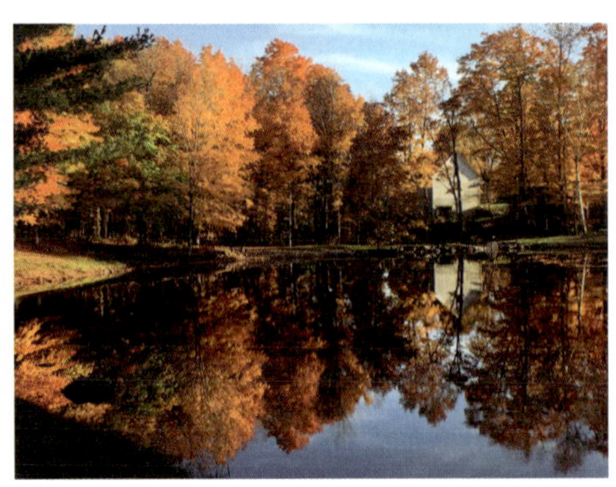

Aglow

'Not my fear, not my fear, ...'
gently flows through
my peaceful musings,
accompanied once again
by a sense of visceral release.
This detached dread
very clearly is not mine.
I know that for sure.
No doubt at all, whatsoever.
As it washes away
inner freedom again expands
that wide open sense of me
as I truly am.
Then ... excitement ... followed by,
or maybe mingled with,
the 'not my fear' undercurrent.
The beauty of it all is that
I know just what to do.
That being, nothing.
Nothing other than breathe and be,
allow my pure and loving essence
to integrate in my now
with Divine comfort distinctly present.
I'm tired,
through and through.
But, I don't care because
partnered with this
fatigue is
a powerful mix of
resilience, hope,

the joy of being me.
These reflections make me feel
aglow
as the coziness of
the sparkling energy
of health
kindles ever more deeply.

October 17, 2019

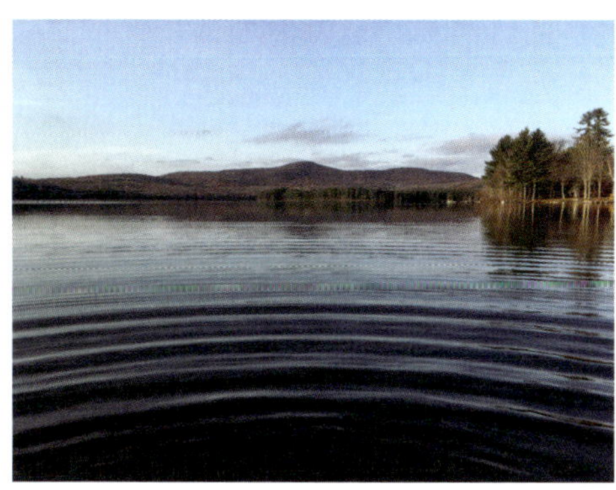

Glorious Ripples

There is such a multidimensional losing
to loss.
One wonders,
"Where did he go? Where am I?
Who am I? Am I okay? How do I go on?"
Slowly, over time, this losing
can turn to finding.
In acknowledging the impact of loss,
it truly is possible to uncover
an eventual sense of gain.
Initially an oppressive weight
that feels immovable and impenetrable,
grief can be an opportunity to
discover one's veritable self
and the value of what ripples
out from within.
As one examines disheveled bits and pieces
of what was once a coherent whole,
there emerges the ability to enable them
to rearrange and reintegrate

in their own way, their own time.
Arriving at this place of
letting go, letting be,
letting in, letting out,
takes time.
And, that's okay.
Instead of heeding the inclinations
to hide or fend off,
there's a sweet liberty
and tangible joy of allowing
one's tenderheartedness to circulate.
Lose, find, heal, be
and you may just make your way to
relishing the reverberations of
your glorious ripples
as they expand
into your surrounds.

November 2, 2019

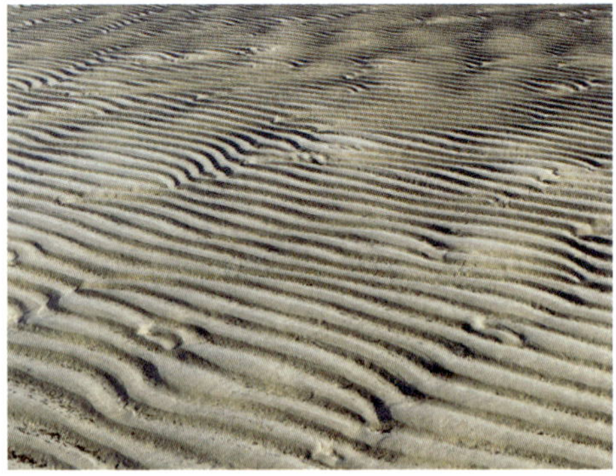

The Nuances of Change

So many transformations in our lives.
Some colossal and life-changing,
others more delicate and quietly altering.
And, of course,
everything in between.
Recently I've been noticing
soft, muted adjustments
in my body, mind, and spirit.
Awareness of these
involves allowing the power of quiet,

floating in the currents of now.
Sometimes this can be a bit disorienting,
though not uncomfortably so.
Patterns of thought,
once valuable and important,
are gently replaced
with novel undulations
of truth.

Singular grains of sand at low tide
nestle together in a splendid,
though temporary,
display.
Each occupies its rightful place
in shared moments of grandeur.
That's the story right there,
right then,
free for beholding.
Just as majestic
is the potential shifting
of the story—
with the winds, the tides,
the drifting of days.
The nuances of change
have a sweet, subtle
radiance of their own.
Recognizing this provides
for ongoing opportunities
to reap the benefits
of the rippling out,
as well as
the rippling in.

November 11, 2019

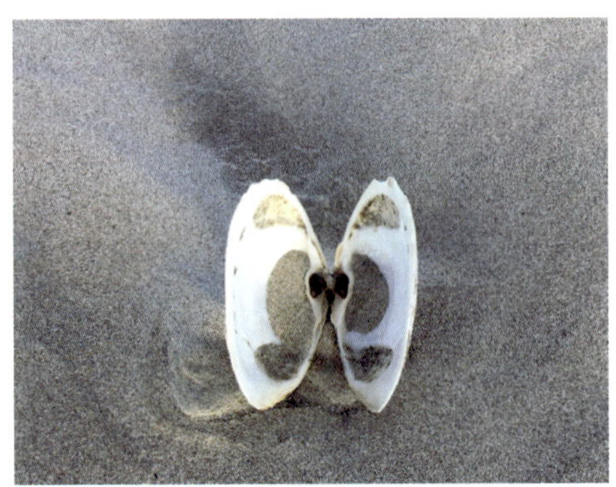

In Tandem

Chest tightens, breath restricts,
unease begins to find a grip.
Wonder surfaces,
"What is that?
Why does it visit?
Should I pay attention, or not?"
And then I choose
the miracle of breath.
That's it.
I just breathe.
As I do, awareness washes in—
this tightness has a narrative
with a very complex plot.
Over time,
these moments of pause
continue to unravel storylines
that make up this life
I have lived so far.
Some I remember vividly,
others remain in a haze.
Some are valid and true,
others imposed and faulty.
What becomes more and more clear
is that the constriction,
though real in the moment,
does not have to honor
stagnant tales of old.
Those struggles are done
if I let them be.
I have the power to

let my story adapt
as I anchor to those
profound undulations
that present themselves
along the way.
Just as love entered my life
exactly when I needed it,
so can I embrace,
even ask for,
Divine love.
I can let the obsolete subplot
of fear and doubt flow away
as many times as necessary.
At the very same time,
I can keep my memories of shared love,
that wonderful sense of being
in tandem,
alive and well within.

November 19, 2019

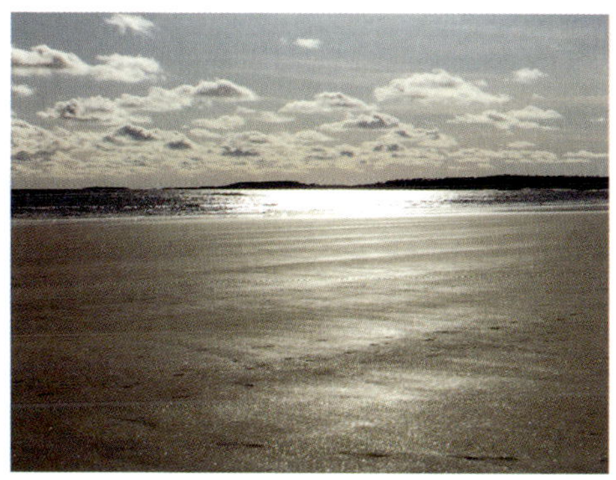

How Big is Your Love?

So much hate all around us.
We experience it
off and on in our own ways,
our own time.
What is hate?
Its synonyms are a yucky bunch:
loathing, detestation, abhorrence,
aversion, animosity, revulsion,
disgust, contempt, abomination.

Such power they have
if allowed, witnessed, received.
Yet, even more powerful is the antonym.
That being, love.
Though hate and all its mates
do exist,
love can be, should be,
stronger.

How big is my love?
Big enough to counteract the hate
that I now understand
was never about me
or because of me.
I know I live from
a place of love,
always have.
I interact, teach, speak, write
from my heart.
The more I recognize that truth,
the more I understand
how monumental love actually is.
As expansive as the sky overhead,
fair weather clouds
gently flowing by.
As immense as a sandy beach
at low tide,
bits of mica sparkling together as one
in the light of a late fall sun.
As vast as the rolling ocean
stretching to places unseen,
reflecting that light from above,
its rhythms a comfort to behold.
As magnanimous as a
generous soul who,
by nature,
loves with a whole heart.

It surely is worth contemplating:
How big is your love?
Can you use it to help counteract
hate and all its mates?

December 1, 2019

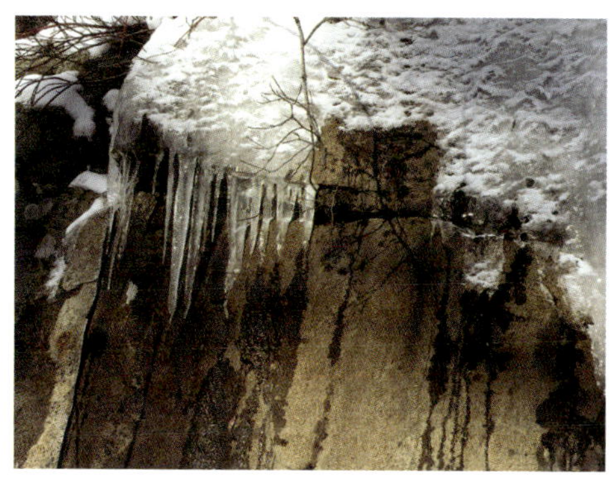

Note to Self

Whenever you feel
that frosty tightness,
just breathe—
through it, with it,
around it, within it.
Warm your wonderful waters
simply by beholding
the beauty of now,
allowing archaic agonies
to soften and drizzle away.
Recognize that
your foundation is strong,
your flow genuine.
Though some shadows remain,
trust that you will attend to them
if need be.
Celebrate the gentle peace
that cascades
through and around you.
Relax into your
uniquely radiant truth.
Live—
be fully alive,
enjoy the joyous rhythms
of omnipresent love.

December 9, 2019

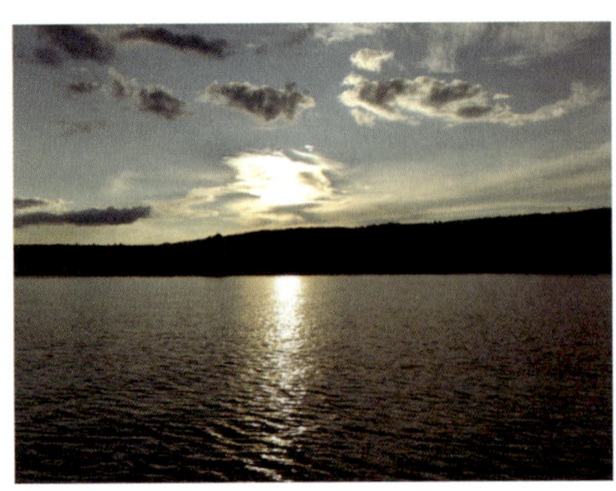

One Love

Imposed angst had a hold
on your good and caring heart.
Little by little you've
found the time and space
to loosen, reclaim, transmute.
You were used to walking hand in hand.
His grip and yours were
gracefully entwined
and you felt safe, held, happy.
You've been reaching,
gingerly trying to take hold,
at the same time
striving to let go
with gentleness and compassion.
You know now that I'm here,
just as you need me to be.
Feel free to take my hand
whenever you need some support.
My light is yours,
your light mine.
Call me whatever you want.
Let go of descriptors
and just feel the love.
It's there, even when it's
a challenge to discern.
My love, his love, her love,
their love, and yours.
It's all the same.

Embrace the essence.
Hold it,
believe it,
cherish it,
walk with it.
It's real and true.
One Love.

December 17, 2019

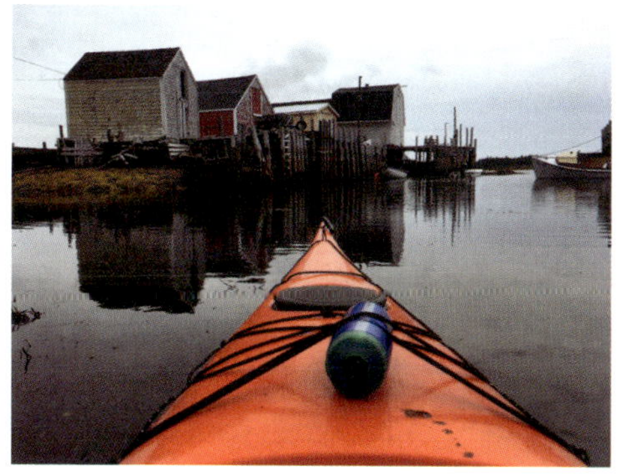

Totally True Reflections

As you sit in the stillness,
recognize that you know
how to move forward,
though the way ahead
may be previously unexplored.
You know when to pause and breathe,
soak in the splendor,
contemplate a challenge.
You have the ability to read the winds,
ride the waves,
paddle strong and steady,
adjust the rudder along the way.
You have what you need on board,
including the freedom
to ask for
and receive help.
You are perfectly human
in your own
wonderfully unique way.

And, yet there's a sameness
in the flow of connection
to others, to nature,
to the Divine.
So, go ahead.
Sit in that stillness.
Let clarity come
in beautiful,
crystal clear,
totally true reflections.
Sit and feel secure
in the solid vessel
that is you.

January 1, 2020

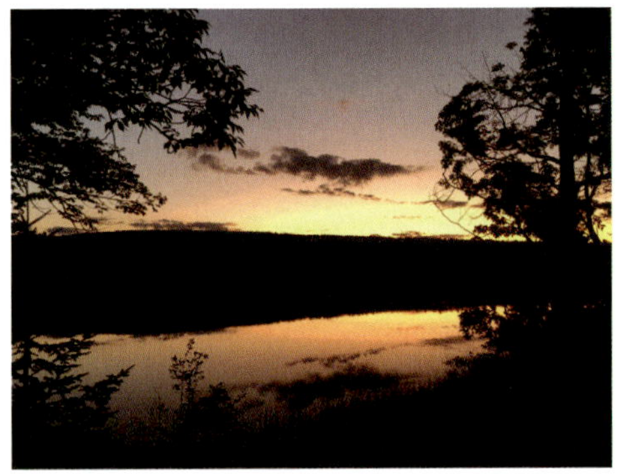

So She Moves

Onward.
A step, a stride, a stance,
a push, a pedal, a pause
at a time.
Relief and renewal
safely nestled within,
solid and secure
she sinks softly
into her own silky waters,
allowing the Light of Love
to enfold her essence.
She smiles
with gentle acceptance
for what has been,

open awareness
of what is now,
lighthearted anticipation
and appreciation
for what will be.
Saturated with a billowing
sense of peace,
inner embers aglow
with eclectic energy and
worldly wisdom—
so she moves ...
onward
with salient, vibrant, radiant
currents of quiet.

January 7, 2020

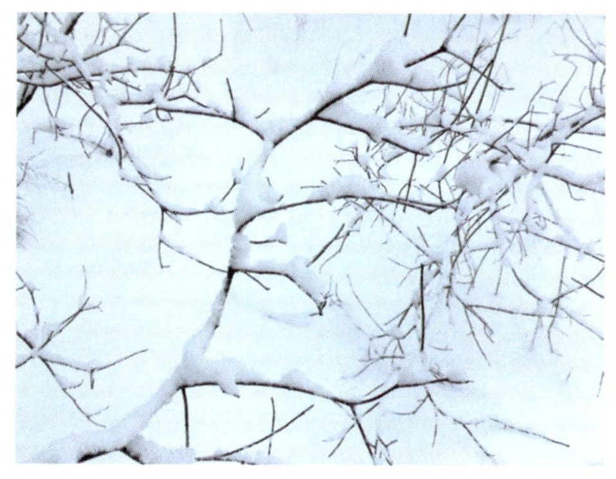

The Delicacy of Softening

Life lesions
leave some parts of us
splintered,
spiky,
silenced.
As those places awaken,
begin to speak,
we must listen
with care,
for they have much
to teach.
A toughness
may have barricaded them,

formed as necessary protection
from the causes
and effects.
This barrier likely
has intricate facets.
As it loosens,
gentleness and kindness
to oneself
is vital.
Inner awareness,
faith in relationship,
belief in one's validity,
are strong company
for the wonder of revival.
As those once sharp,
stiff,
broken places
mellow and mend,
one can appreciate
and welcome
the delicacy of softening.

January 16, 2020
